# MEMPHIS TRAVEL GUIDE

Explore the Iconic Music, Rich History, Mouth-Watering Barbecue, and Outdoor Spaces that Define the Heart & Soul of Memphis

Robert Beauvais

**RB Creative Ink, LLC**

Copyright © 2024 Robert Beauvais

First published by RB Creative Ink, LLC 2024

All rights reserved. No part of this publication may be reproduced, stored or transmitted in any form or by any means, electronic, mechanical, photocopying, recording, scanning, or otherwise without written permission from the publisher. It is illegal to copy this book, post it to a website, or distribute it by any other means without permission.

Robert Beauvais asserts the moral right to be identified as the author of this work.

Robert Beauvais has no responsibility for the persistence or accuracy of URLs for external or third-party Internet Websites referred to in this publication and does not guarantee that any content on such Websites is, or will remain, accurate or appropriate.

Designations used by companies to distinguish their products are often claimed as trademarks. All brand names and product names used in this book and on its cover are trade names, service marks, trademarks and registered trademarks of their respective owners. The publishers and the book are not associated with any product or vendor mentioned in this book. None of the companies referenced within the book have endorsed the book.

First edition

# CONTENTS

Title Page
Copyright
Introduction
Blues & Soul . . . . . . . . . 1
Memphis Rocks . . . . . . . . . 12
Legacy of Justice . . . . . . . . . 22
Taste of Memphis . . . . . . . . . 36
Crafted in Memphis . . . . . . . . . 54
Explore Memphis . . . . . . . . . 70
Beyond the Landmarks . . . . . . . . . 86
Outdoor Adventure . . . . . . . . . 102
Itineraries . . . . . . . . . 120
Conclusion . . . . . . . . . 148
Resources . . . . . . . . . 150

# INTRODUCTION

Memphis, where the rhythm of the Mississippi River meets the soulful sounds of the blues. This city is a place where history is preserved and culture is alive, woven into the very fabric of everyday life. Walking through iconic streets, you'll feel the presence of legends who have shaped Memphis, and the world.

The birthplace of the blues, the home of soul, and the cradle of rock 'n' roll. From Beale Street to Sun Studio, Memphis has witnessed the creation of music that continues to resonate across generations. You'll find yourself following in the footsteps of giants like B.B. King, Elvis Presley, and Otis Redding, whose legacies still echo in every corner of the city.

Memphis also played a pivotal role in the Civil Rights Movement, where some of the most significant moments in American history unfolded. The legacy of leaders like Dr. Martin Luther King Jr. is deeply felt here. It was in Memphis that Dr. King delivered his prophetic "Mountaintop" speech and tragically lost his life while fighting for equal rights. The streets and buildings of Memphis hold stories of struggle, resilience, and triumph, making it a living testament to the ongoing fight for justice and equality.

And then, there's the food. Culinary traditions in Memphis are as rich and storied as the city's musical heritage, and the flavors are as rich as its history. The smoky aroma of slow-cooked barbecue draws you in, inviting you to savor the tastes perfected over generations. But it would be a shame if all you knew about the food scene here was barbecue. So, picture yourself digging into plates of crispy fried catfish, barbecue shrimp, and Southern sides that speak to the heart of comfort food. And don't miss out on trying other local favorites like barbecue spaghetti or the seared scallops at The Beauty Shop—each dish offers a unique taste of Memphis that is sure to impress and beat expectations.

My own journey in Memphis began when I moved here from Anchorage, Alaska—a change that opened up a whole new world of understanding. Memphis captivated me from the start with its music, its barbecue, and its welcoming community. Over the past 20 years, I've developed an intimate and lasting connection to this city. I met the love of my life here, and through her family's generational history in the Mid-South, I've gained a profound appreciation for the culture and history that make Memphis so special.

I wrote this guide for you, to share the things I most enjoy about living in Memphis. No matter what you want to dive into—if you're a music lover, a history buff, or simply curious about the city's rich culture, there is something here for you. Together, we'll explore Memphis's musical roots, visit its civil rights landmarks, taste its amazing food, and uncover some of its hidden gems. Along the way, you'll find practical tips and carefully crafted itineraries designed to help you make the most of your time here. My goal is to help you experience Memphis not just as a destination, but as a living piece of America's cultural heritage.

So, let's embark on this adventure together. The city is waiting for you, and I'm excited to help you uncover all that it has to offer. Now, let's begin our journey with the music that forms the very soul of Memphis. In the first chapter, we'll dive into the rhythms that have shaped the city's identity—blues and soul.

# BLUES & SOUL

*The Rhythms That
Shaped Memphis*

Standing out on the map; Memphis is the bedrock of American music history. With the mournful tunes of the Delta Blues echoing down Beale Street and the ever present sounds of soul music emerging from the city's neighborhoods, Memphis profoundly shaped the nation's soundscape. The journey of these genres is as much a story of migration and transformation as it is of rhythm and melody. In this chapter, we'll explore key sites where this musical history comes alive and offer tips to help you make the most of your visit.

Over the past two decades, I've walked the same streets where legends once played, and felt the echoes of their music in the air. This chapter takes you on a personal journey through the city that has shaped my own love for music. Whether you choose to stroll down Beale Street, immerse yourself in the soulful exhibits at the Stax Museum, or explore the blues roots in neighborhoods across the city, let me guide you, as you discover the rich musical heritage that defines Memphis.

# Beale Street
## *The Heartbeat Of The Blues*

Beale Street—the pulse of Memphis, where the soul of the city comes alive through music, food, and history. Stretching for just under two miles in the heart of downtown, Beale Street has been the epicenter of the city's blues scene for over a century. Here, the blues—carried up from the Mississippi Delta by sharecroppers in search of a better life—found a new home and flourished. The raw, emotive sounds that once echoed from the cotton fields now filled the bars and clubs of Beale Street, offering a sense of hope and resilience to a community facing hardship.

Legends like B.B. King and Muddy Waters first made their mark here, and today, this iconic street continues to buzz with live music every night. With its blend of historic charm and modern energy, Beale Street remains an essential destination for anyone wanting to experience the roots of the blues and the rich culture that defines Memphis.

**When to Visit:** Beale Street is at its best in the evenings, especially on weekends when live music fills the air. However, if you prefer a quieter experience, visit during the daytime to explore the historic sites and shops at a more relaxed pace.

**Parking:** Beale Street turns into a pedestrian corridor on weekends and in the evenings. Parking near Beale Street is not usually a problem. In addition to street parking there are numerous parking garages and surface lots within a few blocks.

**What to Expect:** Beale Street is a lively destination with a mix of music venues, bars, and restaurants. Plan to spend a few hours here, hopping from club to club to catch different live performances. Don't miss renowned spots like B.B. King's Blues Club and Rum Boogie Café.

Beale Street stands as an enduring symbol of Memphis's musical legacy. From its storied past to its lively present, this iconic street offers you a chance to connect with the rhythms that have shaped the city's soul.

*Beale Street*
*https://bealestreet.com/*

# The Blues Hall Of Fame Museum

A short walk from Beale Street, the Blues Hall of Fame celebrates the genre's most influential artists and recordings. This museum is a treasure trove for blues enthusiasts; it's a vital part of preserving the legacy of blues music. The exhibits here offer a detailed look into the lives, struggles, and triumphs of the legends who shaped the genre.

From rare recordings and personal memorabilia to detailed accounts of how the blues evolved and influenced other music styles, the museum provides a comprehensive look at the genre's impact. It's a place where the stories behind the songs come alive, allowing visitors to connect with the cultural and emotional depth of the blues. Throughout the museum, you'll find reminders of how the blues is intertwined with the identity of Memphis, echoing the city's resilience and creative spirit.

**When to Visit:** Weekday mornings or early afternoons are the best times to visit if you want to explore the exhibits without the crowds. The museum occasionally hosts special events, so check their schedule before you go.

**Parking:** There is limited street parking available near the museum. For a more secure and convenient option, park at the National Civil Rights Museum lot, which is just a few blocks away.

**What to Expect:** The Blues Hall of Fame is a smaller, more intimate museum that will take about an hour to explore thoroughly. It's packed with memorabilia, recordings, and personal items from blues legends, offering a glimpse into the genre's history.

Visiting the Blues Hall of Fame Museum offers a glimpse into the past; it's an opportunity to connect with the enduring spirit of the blues and the artists who defined it. Exploring the exhibits, I think you'll gain an increased understanding of the genre's roots and how it influenced Memphis. The music that began as a cry of pain and hope continues to resonate, shaping the city's culture and inspiring new generations of musicians and fans alike.

*Blues Hall of Fame Museum*
*https://blues.org/hall-of-fame-museum/*

# Stax Museum Of American Soul Music

Located on the original site of Stax Records, the Stax Museum of American Soul Music stands as a monument to one of the most influential record labels in history. It was here, in the heart of Memphis, that artists like Otis Redding, Isaac Hayes, and Booker T. & the MG's crafted the soulful sounds that would echo across the globe. Stax Records wasn't just a label; it was a cultural force that gave voice to the African American experience during a pivotal time in American history.

The museum offers a comprehensive look at the history of soul music, tracing its roots in gospel and blues to its profound impact on popular culture. Through exhibits that include rare recordings, vintage instruments, and personal artifacts from the artists themselves, you're invited to explore the moving emotional resonance of soul music. The Stax Museum not only preserves the legacy of these celebrated artists but also tells the broader story of how their music became the soundtrack to a movement for change and equality.

**When to Visit:** The museum is less crowded during weekday mornings, making it an ideal time for a visit. If you're interested in guided tours, check the museum's schedule for dates and times.

**Parking:** The museum has a free parking lot on-site, so you won't have to worry about finding a spot.

**What to Expect:** Plan to spend around 1-2 hours exploring the museum. Highlights include Isaac Hayes' custom Cadillac and the recreated recording studio. The museum offers a chronological journey through the rise of soul music, with plenty of interactive exhibits that bring the era to life.

The Stax Museum is a living testament to the power of music to inspire change. Walking through the museum, you'll feel the spirit of soul music that continues to influence artists and uplift communities around the world. The Stax Museum offers an unforgettable journey into the heart and soul of Memphis music.

*Stax Museum*
*https://staxmuseum.org/*

While exploring the roots of the blues and soul music in Memphis, you'll find that these genres are the heartbeat of a city shaped by its history, struggles, and triumphs. Beale Street's lasting energy, the stories preserved in the Blues Hall of Fame, and the soulful sounds of Stax Records all offer a window into the cultural richness that defines Memphis. These rhythms are woven into the fabric of the city, echoing through its streets, its people, and its enduring legacy of creativity.

The influence of Memphis's blues and soul reaches far beyond the city limits. These sounds have traveled around the globe, inspiring countless artists and movements, while still holding a special place in the heart of Memphis. The music you hear in Memphis today is a living testament to the city's resilience and its ability to transform pain and hope into something beautiful. As you move on to the next chapter, remember that the rhythms of Memphis are not just echoes of the past—they continue to shape the present and future of music.

While blues and soul laid the groundwork, the impact Memphis had on music didn't stop there. In the next chapter, we'll uncover how the city ignited the rock 'n' roll movement, creating a sound that would captivate the world.

# MEMPHIS ROCKS

## *The Birthplace Of Rock 'N' Roll*

**M**emphis is the birthplace of a revolution that changed the world of music forever. The roots of Rock 'n' Roll permeate the city, where the blending of blues, gospel, and country gave rise to a sound that captivated audiences and challenged societal norms. Memphis became the stage for a musical evolution, where innovative artists fused diverse influences to create something entirely new and electrifying.

From the humble beginnings of Sun Studio to the enduring legacy of Rock 'n' Soul, Memphis has been at the heart of Rock 'n' Roll's explosive growth. Exploring these storied sites, you'll gain insight into the creative energy and rebellious spirit that defined an era.

# Rock 'n' Soul Museum

Located on the corner of Beale Street and Third Street, this Smithsonian-affiliated Museum tells the story of how these genres emerged from the rich cultural mix of Memphis. Exploring the Rock 'n' Soul Museum, you'll gain perspective on how blues, gospel, country, and rhythm & blues came together to create a sound that not only shaped the city but also reverberated across the world.

The Rock 'n' Soul Museum stands as a tribute to the creativity and resilience of the musicians who forged new paths in American music. Through detailed exhibits and personal stories, you are invited to experience the struggles and triumphs of the artists who broke barriers and challenged the status quo. The museum showcases the music itself but also the cultural and social environments that influenced its development. Understanding these contexts will help you walk away with an appreciation of how Memphis became a cradle of innovation, where the soul of the nation found its voice.

**When to Visit:** The museum is generally less crowded during weekday mornings, which allows you to explore the exhibits at your own pace. If you want a livelier experience, visiting on a weekend may coincide with special events or temporary exhibitions.

**Parking:** There are several parking options nearby, including the Parking Garage at 149 Peabody Place, just a short walk away. Street parking is also available but can be limited, especially during peak hours.

**What to Expect:** Plan to spend about 1-2 hours here to fully explore the exhibits. The museum offers an audio tour that provides in-depth information, so take advantage of it to enhance your experience. Be prepared for a chronological journey through the development of rock and soul music, with interactive exhibits that bring the stories of the artists and the era to life.

The Rock 'n' Soul Museum is a journey into the soul of a city that shaped the sound of a generation. Experiencing the exhibits, you'll connect with the spirit of innovation and creativity that continues to inspire artists today. This museum stands as a powerful reminder of how music transcends boundaries, bringing people together and influencing the cultural landscape long after the first notes are played.

*Rock 'n' Soul Museum*
*https://www.memphisrocknsoul.org/*

# Sun Studio
## *The Birthplace of Rock 'n' Roll*

Sun Studio is widely regarded as the birthplace of Rock 'n' Roll, and its legacy is etched into the annals of music history. This small, unassuming building on Union Avenue became the launching pad for some of the most influential artists of all time—Elvis Presley, Johnny Cash, Carl Perkins, and Jerry Lee Lewis, among others. The recordings made within these walls set the stage for a musical revolution that would sweep the globe and forever alter the course of popular music.

Despite its modest size, Sun Studio has retained much of its vintage charm, offering visitors an opportunity to step back in time and experience the magic of those early recording sessions. As you walk through the doors, you can almost hear the echoes of the music that shaped a generation and feel the raw energy that fueled the birth of Rock 'n' Roll. Visiting Sun Studio is like touching the very roots of modern music, where innovation and rebellion converged to create something truly groundbreaking.

> **When to Visit:** The studio is open for tours daily, but to avoid the busiest times, consider visiting early in the morning or late in the afternoon. Evening tours are also quieter and often provide a more intimate atmosphere to explore the studio.

**Parking:** There is a small parking lot available at Sun Studio, but it can fill up quickly. Street parking is also an option, though it may require a short walk. Alternatively, there is a paid, lot at the corner of Orleans and Monroe.

**What to Expect:** The guided tour lasts about an hour and is packed with fascinating stories and insights about the artists who recorded here. You'll see original recording equipment, hear clips from incredible sessions, and even stand on the very spot where Elvis recorded his first song. Be sure to browse the gift shop for unique memorabilia before you leave.

Sun Studio stands as a living testament to the origins of Rock 'n' Roll, continuing to inspire both artists and fans. A visit here offers a rare opportunity to connect with the sounds and stories that revolutionized the music world. Sun Studio provides an experience that resonates long after you leave.

*Sun Studio*
*https://www.sunstudio.com/*

# Graceland
## *Elvis Presley's Mansion*

Graceland is the ultimate destination for Elvis fans, and anyone interested in the legacy of the King of Rock 'n' Roll. Located just a short drive from downtown Memphis, this world renowned mansion offers a glimpse into the life of Elvis Presley, from his luxurious living spaces to his personal collection of memorabilia. The self-guided tour takes you through several rooms of the mansion, including the famous Jungle Room, and ends with a visit to the Meditation Garden, where Elvis and his family are laid to rest. For a more immersive experience, consider the VIP tour, which offers access to exclusive exhibits and a more personalized visit.

Graceland is a pilgrimage site that draws fans from around the world, offering a personal connection to the life and career of a music legend. The mansion provides a window into the world of Elvis, from the opulent décor to the one-of-a-kind artifacts that tell the story of his rise to fame and enduring influence on the world of music. Visiting Graceland, you will explore the history of the site and step into the world of Elvis to experience the legacy of a cultural icon.

> **When to Visit:** Graceland is open year-round, but weekdays are generally less crowded. If you want to avoid the largest crowds, plan your visit in the early morning or late afternoon.

**Parking:** Graceland offers on-site parking for a fee, and there's ample space available. If you're visiting during peak times, plan to arrive early to secure a spot.

**What to Expect:** The standard mansion tour lasts about 1.5 to 2 hours, but you can easily spend more time exploring the additional exhibits and museums on the property. For instance, Elvis' famous Pink Cadilac can be seen at the Presley Motors Automobile Museum located on the grounds.

Exploring Graceland is an immersive journey into the life of Elvis Presley. Walking through the rooms where he lived and created music, I expect you'll learn something new about his influence on both popular culture and the music industry. Graceland provides a rare opportunity to connect with the legacy of the King, whose impact continues to resonate across generations.

*Graceland*
*https://www.graceland.com/*

Immersing yourself in the history of Rock 'n' Roll, you'll uncover the stories and places that ignited a musical revolution. From the humble beginnings at Sun Studio to the cultural impact preserved at Graceland, Memphis stands as a testament to the creativity and rebellious spirit that defined an era. These visits will connect you with the power and innovation that continue to influence music today.

Memphis's role in the birth of Rock 'n' Roll is the foundation of a genre that has shaped the soundscape of the world. The music born in this city transcended boundaries, inspired movements, and created legends. As you move on to explore other aspects of Memphis's rich cultural heritage, remember that the spirit of Rock 'n' Roll is alive and well, still echoing through the streets of the city where it all began.

Having explored how Memphis music shaped the world, we must also remember that this city has been a powerful stage in the fight for justice and equality. In the next chapter, we'll walk through the city's civil rights landmarks, where the struggle for freedom left an indelible mark on history.

If you're enjoying this guide and finding it informative and helpful, I would greatly appreciate it if you could take a moment to leave a review on Amazon. Your feedback helps other travelers discover the unique charm of Memphis and ensures this guide continues to serve those looking to explore the city. Thank you for being a part of this journey!

 *Amazon Link: Memphis Travel Guide*
*https://www.amazon.com/dp/ B0DGTS1CH8/*

❖ ❖ ❖

# LEGACY OF JUSTICE

*Civil Rights Landmarks*

Memphis has been a cornerstone of American history, not only through its music but also as a pivotal battleground in the Civil Rights Movement. The city's landmarks stand as powerful reminders of the courage and determination of those who fought for justice and equality. Walking through these sites is an emotional journey that connects the past to the present, reminding us of the progress made and the work still to be done.

I've often found myself emotionally moved by these sites, reflecting on their significance and the stories they hold. In this chapter I invite you to step into the city's history, to see where pivotal moments unfolded and to feel the weight of a legacy that continues to shape our world today.

# National Civil Rights Museum
## *The Lorraine Motel*

The National Civil Rights Museum, located at the historic Lorraine Motel, stands as one of the most significant landmarks in American history. Another Smithsonian Affiliate, the museum offers an unparalleled educational experience, drawing on the vast resources and expertise of the Smithsonian Institution. This site houses a comprehensive museum dedicated to the Civil Rights Movement and preserves the very place where Dr. Martin Luther King Jr. was assassinated on April 4, 1968.

The museum takes visitors on an emotional journey through civil rights history, with exhibits spanning from the early days of slavery to the ongoing struggle for equality. Experiencing the museum's powerful exhibits, you'll encounter the preserved exterior of the Lorraine Motel, complete with the vintage cars and nationally recognized facade that evoke the era. Standing before Room 306, where Dr. King spent his final moments, is a profoundly moving experience, bringing the gravity of the Civil Rights Movement into stark relief. This combined visit offers an opportunity to connect with the past, reflect on the progress, and recognize the work that lies ahead in the fight for justice and equality.

**When to Visit:** The museum is busiest on weekends and during the late morning, so consider visiting early on a weekday to explore the exhibits at your own pace. Special events and guided tours are often available, so it's worth checking the museum's schedule for these details.

**Parking:** There is a parking lot adjacent to the museum with ample space, but it can fill up during peak times. Additional parking is available on nearby streets, be prepared to walk a short distance.

**What to Expect:** Plan to spend at least 2-3 hours at the museum to fully absorb the exhibits. The experience is immersive and can be emotionally intense, so allow yourself time to reflect.

Visiting the National Civil Rights Museum at the historic Lorraine Motel is an experience that connects you to the struggles and triumphs that have shaped the fight for justice and equality, not only in Memphis but in America. This site serves as a powerful reminder that the fight for civil rights continues to resonate in today's world. As you leave, I encourage you to carry with you a deeper understanding of the Civil Rights Movement and its enduring impact, inspiring you to contribute to the ongoing pursuit of equality in your own way.

*National Civil Rights Museum*
*https://www.civilrightsmuseum.org/*

# Mason Temple
## *The Mountaintop Speech*

Mason Temple holds a profound place in the history of the Civil Rights Movement, as the site where Dr. Martin Luther King Jr. delivered his prophetic "I've Been to the Mountaintop" speech on the evening of April 3, 1968. This address, given just one day before his assassination at the Lorraine Motel, stands as one of the most powerful and poignant speeches in American history. In it, Dr. King reflects on the struggles and progress of the movement, speaking with an eerie foresight about his own mortality and the future of the fight for equality.

The speech is remembered not only for its eloquence and passion but also for the sense of urgency and reflection it conveyed. Standing in the very sanctuary where Dr. King delivered these historic words allows visitors to feel the weight of that moment and the enduring impact of his message. The temple's preservation of this legacy makes it a sacred space where the past resonates with the present, reminding us of the ongoing journey toward justice and equality.

> **When to Visit:** Mason Temple is an active church, so it's best to check ahead for visiting hours. If possible, align your visit with a service or special event to experience the building in use, as it was when Dr. King spoke there.

**Parking:** The church has a parking lot available for visitors. I recommend visiting Mason Temple after your trip to the National Civil Rights Museum. It's only a 10-minute drive from the museum and is an impactful way to wrap up your experience.

**What to Expect:** Visitors should plan to spend about 30 minutes to an hour at Mason Temple, allowing time to reflect in the sanctuary where Dr. King delivered his final speech. Guided tours may be available, and it's recommended to check the temple's website in advance for event and tour schedule information to enhance your visit.

A visit to Mason Temple offers a direct connection to Dr. King's legacy and the Civil Rights Movement. Standing in the same sanctuary where his powerful words resonated, reflect on the courage and vision that fueled the fight for justice. This experience not only complements your visit to the National Civil Rights Museum and the Lorraine Motel but also enriches your understanding of the enduring impact of Dr. King's message on our world today.

*Mason Temple*
*https://tinyurl.com/mason-temple*

# WDIA
## Radio Station Marquee

The original site of WDIA Radio Station at 112 Union Ave is a landmark in American broadcasting history, known as the first radio station in the United States to feature an all-Black format. Launched in 1948, WDIA quickly became a voice for the African American community, not only in Memphis but across the nation, as its signal reached listeners from Tennessee to the Mississippi Delta. Although the station is no longer located at this address, the original WDIA marquee and a historical marker remain as powerful symbols of WDIA's enduring legacy.

WDIA played a crucial role in promoting blues, gospel, and R&B music, genres that were often overlooked by mainstream media at the time. Beyond its musical contributions, WDIA was a platform for addressing important social issues, from civil rights to community concerns. The station's influence helped to elevate Black voices and stories at a time when they were often marginalized, making it a symbol of both Memphis's and the nation's cultural history.

> **When to Visit:** The site is an outdoor landmark, so you can visit at any time. Early mornings or late afternoons are ideal for taking photos without the midday glare. Consider grabbing a bite at Huey's, located at the end of the block—just look for the green and white signature awnings.

**Parking:** Street parking is available near the site, but spaces can be limited during peak hours. Consider parking in a nearby lot or garage and walking.

**What to Expect:** As a historical marker rather than a traditional museum, the visit is brief but meaningful. Take a moment to reflect on the station's influence and how it gave a voice to those who were often unheard.

While the visit itself may be short, the impact of WDIA's contributions to music and civil rights continues to resonate. Reflecting on the station's role in amplifying Black voices and shaping cultural narratives, you'll leave with a greater appreciation for its place in the broader story of Memphis and the Civil Rights Movement.

 *WDIA Radio Station Marquee*
*https://tinyurl.com/wdia-radio-marquee*

# Clayborn Temple
## *I Am A Man Plaza*

Known for its pivotal role in the Memphis sanitation workers' strike, February 12, 1968, Clayborn Temple is another site with significant civil rights connections. This historic church became a central hub for organizing and inspiring the movement, where the famous "I Am A Man" signs were created and distributed, symbolizing the fight for dignity, respect, and equality. The strike, which was sparked after two sanitation workers were tragically killed, became a turning point in the Civil Rights Movement, drawing national attention and ultimately leading to Dr. Martin Luther King Jr.'s involvement in Memphis.

Adjacent to the temple is the I Am A Man Plaza, a public space dedicated to commemorating the courage and resilience of the sanitation workers and their struggle for civil rights. The plaza features a powerful sculpture that echoes the phrase "I Am A Man," serving as a lasting reminder of the ongoing quest for justice. Together, Clayborn Temple and I Am A Man Plaza offer visitors an impactful connection to this pivotal moment in history, highlighting the enduring fight for equality.

**When to Visit:** Both Clayborn Temple and I Am A Man Plaza are open to the public, making them accessible for visits at any time. However, visiting during daylight hours is recommended to fully appreciate the site's significance and the detailed artwork in the plaza. Consider combining your visit with a walk around the nearby South Main Historic District, where you can explore other important Civil Rights sites.

**Parking:** Street parking is available near the temple and plaza, though it can be limited during busy times. Additional parking can be found in nearby lots, especially if you're planning to explore the surrounding area.

**What to Expect:** The temple itself may be viewed from the outside, check the website for tours and events. The outdoor plaza invites visitors to engage with its public art and historical markers. Plan to spend about 30 minutes to an hour here, allowing time to absorb the significance of this important site.

A visit to Clayborn Temple and I Am A Man Plaza offers a powerful and reflective experience, connecting you to the legacy of the 1968 sanitation workers' strike and the larger Civil Rights Movement. Plan to spend about 30 minutes to an hour here, allowing time to fully absorb the significance of this important site and its ongoing relevance in the fight for justice.

*I Am A Man Plaza*
*https://tinyurl.com/i-am-a-man-plaza*

E xploring these civil rights landmarks in Memphis will take you on a journey through history and provide the opportunity to connect with stories of courage, resilience, and the relentless pursuit of justice. Each site, from the National Civil Rights Museum at the Lorraine Motel to Mason Temple, offers a powerful reminder of the sacrifices made and the progress achieved in the struggle for equality.

These landmarks are living reminders that the fight for civil rights continues. Your visit to these sites is a chance to reflect on key events and to be inspired by the legacy of those who came before us. As you continue to explore Memphis, I encourage you to let the lessons learned and the stories heard motivate you to contribute to the continued pursuit of equality in your own life and community.

With the powerful history of civil rights still fresh in our minds, let's shift focus to another cornerstone of Memphis culture—its food. In the next chapter, we'll savor the flavors that make this city's culinary scene as memorable as its music and its enduring march toward equality.

# TASTE OF MEMPHIS

*Barbecue &
Local Favorites*

When it comes to food, Memphis has long traditions of bold flavors, with barbecue being a central part of its identity. The smoky, tender meats that define Memphis-style barbecue are a source of pride for locals and a must-try for visitors. While barbecue is the city's signature dish, there's a wide array of other mouth-watering options that reflect the diverse influences that have shaped Memphis over the years. Soul food staples like fried catfish and banana pudding are local favorites, along with creative dishes that blend traditional Southern ingredients with global flavors.

In this chapter, we'll take you on a journey through some of the best places to eat in Memphis, highlighting my favorite barbecue spots and local favorites that offer a true taste of the city. Whether you're indulging in the ribs at The Bar-B-Q Shop, savoring the sweet and savory dishes at The Beauty Shop, or enjoying a nostalgic treat at A. Schwab's soda fountain, you'll see how Memphis cuisine is as diverse and interesting as the city itself. So come hungry and get ready to explore the flavors that make Memphis a food lover's paradise.

# The Bar-B-Q Shop

The Bar-B-Q Shop is a personal favorite, known far and wide for its award-winning barbecue and distinctive offerings that set it apart from the competition. Located in the heart of Midtown, this family-owned restaurant has been serving up smoky, flavorful barbecue since the early 1980s. The warm, inviting atmosphere and the mouth-watering aroma of slow-cooked meats make it a must-visit for both locals and tourists alike. Over the years, The Bar-B-Q Shop has garnered a loyal following, thanks in large part to its signature dishes that blend traditional Memphis flavors with a creative twist.

One of the standout items on the menu is the Barbecue Spaghetti, a dish that perfectly exemplifies the restaurant's innovative approach to classic Southern cuisine. Alongside their famous ribs, which are cooked to tender perfection and basted in a rich, tangy sauce, the Barbecue Spaghetti has become a beloved staple for those seeking something different. Whether you're a first-time visitor or a regular, The Bar-B-Q Shop offers a memorable meal that captures the essence of Memphis barbecue.

**Parking:** The Bar-B-Q Shop has a small parking lot in the back, but it can fill up quickly during peak times. Street parking is also available in the surrounding neighborhood, though you may need to walk a short distance.

**Cost:** Meals at The Bar-B-Q Shop are reasonably priced, with most dishes ranging from $10 to $25. The generous portions and exceptional quality make it a great value for anyone looking to enjoy authentic Memphis barbecue.

A visit to The Bar-B-Q Shop is an experience that embodies the rich barbecue tradition of Memphis. With its cozy atmosphere, innovative dishes, and unbeatable flavors, this spot is a must-visit for anyone looking to savor the true taste of Memphis. Be sure to try the ribs and Barbecue Spaghetti—you won't be disappointed.

 *The Bar-B-Q Shop*
*https://thebar-b-qshop.com/*

# Blues City Café

Blues City Café, located on iconic Beale Street, has been a staple of the Memphis food scene since it opened its doors in 1991. Known for its lively atmosphere and mouth-watering barbecue, this café perfectly captures the spirit of Memphis. The moment you step inside, you're greeted by the aroma of slow-cooked meats and the sound of live blues music, creating an unforgettable dining experience. Blues City Café is a celebration of Memphis's rich cultural heritage, where food and music come together in perfect harmony.

The menu is packed with Southern favorites, but the standout dishes are undoubtedly the barbecue ribs, Barbecue Shrimp, and the famous tamales. The ribs are slow-cooked, falling off the bone with each bite, while the Barbecue Shrimp is a savory dish bursting with flavor. The tamales, a hidden gem on the menu, offer a delightful twist with their rich, spiced filling wrapped in tender cornmeal. All these dishes are served with classic Southern sides, making Blues City Café a must-visit spot for anyone looking to indulge in authentic Memphis cuisine.

> **Parking:** Beale street is often closed to vehicle traffic, especially during peak hours, but there is ample parking nearby. The Beale Street Parking Garage is a convenient option, as well as surface lots and street parking.

**Cost:** Meals at Blues City Café are moderately priced, with most dishes ranging from $12 to $25. The lively atmosphere and generous portions make it well worth the visit.

Blues City Café offers an authentic taste of Memphis, with its standout barbecue dishes and vibrant atmosphere. Whether you live here or are visiting, this café is the perfect place to experience the flavors and sounds that make Beale Street legendary. Don't miss out on the barbecue ribs and Barbecue Shrimp—they're the stars of the menu.

*Blues City Café*
*https://bluescitycafé.com/*

# The Arcade Restaurant

The Arcade Restaurant is a portrait of Memphis's history, known as the city's oldest café, having served the community since 1919. Located in the historic South Main Arts District, the Arcade's retro vibe, complete with vintage décor and a classic diner feel, transports visitors back in time. A favorite haunt of Elvis Presley, the restaurant even has a designated table where the King himself often dined, adding a touch of rock 'n' roll history to your visit.

While the Memphis Belle Pie is a must-try dessert, the Arcade is also famous for its hearty Southern dishes. Named after the World War II B-17 bomber, the pie is a decadent blend of chocolate, pecans, and other Southern flavors. For breakfast, the sweet potato pancakes are a standout, offering a delicious start to your day. If you're visiting for lunch or dinner, the country-fried steak with gravy is a classic choice, providing a true taste of Southern comfort food that keeps diners coming back.

> **Parking:** Parking is available around the South Main Arts District, with both metered street parking and nearby lots. During peak times, finding a spot can be challenging, so plan to arrive a bit early.

**Cost:** Meals at the Arcade are reasonably priced, with most dishes ranging from $8 to $15. You'll find good value for the classic dishes served here no matter when you visit.

Dining at the Arcade Restaurant is a journey through Memphis's past, where history and flavor come together in a cozy, nostalgic setting. Whether you're there for breakfast, lunch, or dinner, the Arcade offers a true taste of Southern comfort food in an atmosphere rich with stories from the city's history.

*The Arcade Restaurant*
*https://arcaderestaurant.com/*

# The Beauty Shop

The Beauty Shop is a unique and trendy dining spot in the Cooper-Young neighborhood, where history meets modern culinary innovation. Once a 1950s beauty salon, this space has been transformed into a chic restaurant while retaining much of its original charm. You can still see the vintage hairdryers and retro décor, which add a quirky yet nostalgic vibe to the dining experience. The brainchild of renowned chef Karen Carrier, The Beauty Shop is known for its eclectic menu that fuses global flavors with Southern roots, offering a dining experience that's as stylish as it is delicious.

One of the standout dishes is the Bread Pudding, a dessert that has become a favorite among locals and visitors alike, but The Beauty Shop's menu has much more to offer. For brunch, the watermelon and wings dish is a refreshing and flavorful combination that showcases Chef Karen's creativity. For dinner, the seared scallops with sweet potato puree and applewood-smoked bacon is a must-try, perfectly balancing savory and sweet flavors in a dish that's as beautiful as it is satisfying.

> **Parking:** Parking in the Cooper-Young isn't usually a problem. Street parking is available on the numerous side streets, but you may need to walk a block or two. There's also a nearby lot that can be used by restaurant patrons, regardless of which restaurant you choose to visit.

**Cost:** The Beauty Shop is an upscale dining experience, with prices reflecting the quality and creativity of the dishes. Expect to pay between $15 and $35 for most entrees, with brunch items generally on the lower end of that range.

The Beauty Shop offers a dining experience you're likely not to find anywhere else, combining history, style, and exceptional cuisine. Whether you're stopping by for a leisurely brunch or an elegant dinner, you'll find something special on the menu that reflects the creative flair of Chef Karen Carrier.

 *The Beauty Shop Restaurant*
*https://thebeautyshoprestaurant.com/*

# The Four Way

The Four Way is a living piece of Memphis history. Established in 1946, The Four Way quickly became a gathering place of the South Memphis community and played a significant role during the Civil Rights Movement. Leaders like Dr. Martin Luther King Jr. and other prominent activists often gathered here to discuss strategy and enjoy a hearty meal. The restaurant's ties to the Civil Rights era are felt throughout, making it a place where history and tradition are served alongside soul food classics.

The menu at The Four Way is filled with comforting Southern dishes that have stood the test of time. Among the highlights is their Banana Pudding, a dessert that perfectly captures the sweet, home-cooked flavors of the South. For a true taste of Memphis, try the fried catfish or the smothered pork chops, both served with traditional sides like collard greens and cornbread. These dishes satisfy your appetite and connect you to the rich cultural and historical legacy of the restaurant.

**Parking:** The Four Way offers a small parking lot for customers, but it can fill up quickly, especially during lunch hours. Additional street parking is available nearby, though it may require a short walk.

**Cost:** The Four Way is known for its reasonable prices, with most meals ranging from $8 to $15. The generous portions and soulful flavors make it a great value for anyone looking to experience authentic Southern cooking.

The Four Way is a cultural landmark that continues to serve the Memphis community with pride. A visit to The Four Way offers a meaningful and delicious experience as well as a historical connection to the city's heritage.

*The Four Way Restaurant*
*https://www.fourway901.com/*

# Elwood's Shack

Elwood's Shack is a true hidden gem in Memphis, beloved by locals for its down-to-earth vibe and seriously good food. Located in a humble building near the edge of town, this unassuming spot has earned a reputation for serving up some of the best selections of smoked meats and Southern comfort dishes in the city. The laid-back atmosphere, complete with picnic tables and a no-frills approach, makes Elwood's Shack a go-to for anyone looking to enjoy a casual, satisfying meal without the fuss.

The menu at Elwood's Shack is packed with flavorful dishes that showcase the rich traditions of Southern cooking. The smoked brisket and pulled pork are crowd favorites, each served with a side of house-made coleslaw and baked beans. For breakfast lovers, the smoked salmon bagel is a surprising standout, offering a local twist on a classic dish. No matter when you visit, Elwood's Shack promises a satisfying meal that captures the essence of local Memphis food.

> **Parking:** Parking at Elwood's Shack can be a bit unconventional since it shares a lot with Lowe's. There's usually plenty of space, but it's worth noting that the restaurant doesn't have a dedicated parking area.

**Cost:** Meals at Elwood's Shack are reasonably priced, with most dishes ranging from $10 to $15. The generous portions and high quality make it a great value for those looking to enjoy low-key dining experience.

Elwood's Shack is a must-visit for anyone seeking a casual, authentic Memphis dining experience. With its unpretentious setting and mouth-watering dishes, it's the perfect spot to enjoy some of the best barbecue and Southern fare the city has to offer.

*Elwood's Shack*
*https://www.elwoodsshack.com/*

# A. Schwab
## *Soda Fountain*

A. Schwab is a Beale Street landmark that has been a part of Memphis's history since 1876. Known for its eclectic mix of goods, this old-fashioned dry goods store offers everything from vintage clothing to quirky souvenirs. But one of the most charming features of A. Schwab is its vintage soda fountain, which transports visitors back to a bygone era. Whether you're grabbing a classic soda or indulging in an ice cream sundae, the soda fountain at A. Schwab is a nostalgic experience that captures the spirit of old Memphis.

The soda fountain, restored to its former glory, serves up a delightful array of traditional treats that are hard to find elsewhere. From root beer floats to malts and milkshakes made with hand-dipped ice cream, each item is a sweet taste of the past. It's the perfect spot to take a break from exploring Beale Street, offering a refreshing and fun way to experience a piece of Memphis history.

> **Parking:** Beale street is often closed to vehicle traffic, especially during peak hours, but there is ample parking nearby. A. Schwab is best visited during daylight hours to take in the historic building in the natural light.

**Cost:** The items at the soda fountain are reasonably priced, with most treats costing between $3 and $6. It's an affordable way to enjoy a sweet break during your visit to Beale Street.

A visit to A. Schwab's soda fountain is a step back in time, offering a charming and nostalgic experience in the heart of Beale Street. Whether you're stopping in for a quick treat or soaking up the vintage vibes, it's a delightful addition to any Memphis itinerary.

 *A. Schwab*
*https://tinyurl.com/soda-fountain*

These culinary experiences are a gateway to understanding the heart and soul of Memphis. From the time-honored traditions of Memphis-style barbecue to the soul-satisfying dishes found in local haunts, each meal tells a story of the city's heritage and its people. Whether you're indulging in the smoky perfection of ribs at The Bar-B-Q Shop or savoring the one-of-a-kind flavors at The Beauty Shop, these are just a sampling of the establishments and food that make Memphis special.

Each restaurant, each dish, is a chapter in the story of Memphis—a story of resilience, creativity, and an unwavering love for good food. So, bring your appetite and get ready to savor the flavors that make Memphis a culinary destination like no other.

Having delighted in Memphis's barbecue and other Southern dishes, it's time to raise a glass to the city's flourishing craft beverage scene. Next, we'll explore the local breweries and distilleries that add a distinctive flavor to Memphis's rich culinary heritage.

# CRAFTED IN MEMPHIS

*BREWERIES & DISTILLERIES*

Attracting a passionate following, Memphis's craft brewing and distilling culture is steeped in rich history and ongoing traditions. In recent years, local breweries and distilleries have flourished, offering an array of interesting and flavorful drinks that embody the city's spirit. Whether you're seeking a cold, refreshing beer or a finely crafted whiskey, there's something special waiting for you.

This chapter will take you on a journey through some of the city's standout breweries and distilleries. From the inventive beers at Wiseacre Brewing Company to the expertly distilled Blue Note Bourbon at B.R. Distilling Company, you'll experience the creativity and craftsmanship that make Memphis a destination for beverage enthusiasts. So, get ready to explore the flavors that make this city's craft scene truly remarkable.

# Wiseacre Brewing Company

With a reputation built on creativity and innovation, Wiseacre combines traditional brewing techniques with bold, modern flavors. Brothers Davin and Kellan Bartosch founded the brewery in 2013, and their distinctive approach has quickly made it a standout in the industry. The brewery's offerings include the popular Tiny Bomb American Pilsner, a crisp and refreshing beer that has become a local favorite, and the Gotta Get Up to Get Down Coffee Milk Stout, which showcases the depth and variety of their craft.

With its lively atmosphere and commitment to quality, Wiseacre has become a must-visit destination for beer enthusiasts. The brewery's focus on community and creativity is evident in every aspect, from the myriad brews to the welcoming taproom. Whether you're a seasoned beer lover or just curious to explore Memphis's craft scene, Wiseacre offers an experience that's both satisfying and memorable.

> **When to Visit:** Wiseacre Brewing Company is open throughout the week, with extended hours on weekends. On weekends, the brewery comes alive with special events, food trucks, and occasional live music. Check their calendar for upcoming tours, beer releases, and events to enhance your visit.

**Parking:** There is a dedicated parking lot at the brewery, but it can fill up quickly, especially during peak hours. Street parking is also available in the surrounding area, though it may require a short walk.

**What to Expect:** Expect a laid-back, welcoming atmosphere with a spacious taproom and outdoor seating. Wiseacre often hosts local food trucks, making it easy to grab a bite while you enjoy your beer. The brewery is family-friendly and dog-friendly, creating a community vibe that's perfect for a casual outing or a gathering with friends.

A visit to Wiseacre Brewing Company is a chance to immerse yourself in the spirit of Memphis's craft culture. With its variety of brews and lively atmosphere, Wiseacre provides a true taste of what makes Memphis special.

*Wiseacre Brewing*
*https://wiseacrebrew.com/*

# Memphis Made Brewing Company

Known for its small-batch, handcrafted beers, Memphis Made Brewing Company captures the spirit of Memphis. Founded in 2013 by Andy Ashby and Drew Barton, this brewery has become a staple of the Cooper-Young neighborhood, a hub of creativity and community in Memphis. Their approach to brewing is grounded in originality and craftsmanship, with a rotating selection of seasonal brews. Popular offerings like Fireside Amber Ale and Parkways Session IPA reflect their commitment to producing high-quality beers that cater to a variety of tastes.

The brewery's cozy taproom and inviting outdoor patio provide the perfect setting to enjoy their craft beers. Memphis Made is a community gathering spot where locals come together to enjoy great beer, live music, and the occasional food truck. Memphis Made offers an authentic taste of the city's craft beer culture.

**When to Visit:** Memphis Made Brewing Co. is open most days of the week, with longer hours on weekends. Saturdays often feature events like beer releases or local markets, which can add to the experience.

**Parking:** Parking in the Cooper-Young isn't usually a problem. Street parking is available on the numerous side streets, but you may need to walk a block or two.

**What to Expect:** Memphis Made often hosts local food trucks, live music, and community events, creating a lively atmosphere. The brewery is also dog-friendly, so feel free to bring your furry friends along.

A visit to Memphis Made Brewing Company offers a chance to experience the warmth and creativity of the Cooper-Young neighborhood. With its refreshing brews and welcoming atmosphere, Memphis Made is a highly recommended destination for anyone looking to immerse themselves in the local craft beer scene.

*Memphis Made Brewing https:// www.memphismadebrewing.com/*

# Ghost River Brewing Company

Ghost River Brewing Company is a pioneer in Memphis's craft beer scene, established in 2007. Located in the South Main Arts District, this brewery is named after the Ghost River section of the Wolf River, from which it sources its water. This connection to local resources and a commitment to sustainability are reflected in their beers, which have become staples in the Memphis community. Signature brews like the Golden Ale and Grindhouse Cream Ale showcase the brewery's dedication to quality and tradition, making Ghost River a key player in the Memphis craft beer landscape.

The brewery's taproom offers a welcoming space to enjoy their wide variety of beers, many of which are available exclusively on-site. With a laid-back atmosphere and a spacious outdoor patio, Ghost River is the perfect spot to relax and enjoy a drink, especially during the warmer months. The brewery frequently hosts live music, food trucks, and community events, making it a popular gathering place for both locals and visitors.

**When to Visit:** Ghost River Brewing Co. is open daily, with extended hours on weekends. Check their calendar for special events or brewery tours.

**Parking:** The brewery has a small parking lot, which tends to fill up quickly, especially during busy times. Street parking is available in the surrounding area, and there are several public parking lots within walking distance.

**What to Expect:** Ghost River's taproom offers a warm, inviting atmosphere with a variety of beers on tap, many of which are only available at the brewery. The outdoor patio is a great spot to enjoy a drink, especially during the warmer months. Community events, live music and food trucks are common on the weekends.

A visit to Ghost River Brewing Company provides an authentic taste of Memphis, combining locally sourced ingredients with an ingrained sense of community. As you enjoy a pint in the taproom or on the patio, you'll find that Ghost River offers a true reflection of the city's craft beer culture.

*Ghost River Brewing*
*https://www.ghostriverbrewing.com/*

# High Cotton Brewing Company

High Cotton Brewing Company is a pillar of Memphis's craft beer scene, known for its dedication to traditional brewing techniques and high-quality craftsmanship. Founded in 2013, High Cotton is located in the bustling Edge District and has built a reputation for producing beers that honor classic styles with a touch of Southern charm. Brews like the rich, malty Scottish Ale and the crisp, refreshing Belgian Wit reflect the brewery's commitment to excellence and its appreciation for time-honored brewing methods.

The brewery's rustic taproom and cozy outdoor patio provide an inviting atmosphere for enjoying a pint. High Cotton is also known for its community involvement, frequently hosting charity fundraisers and local events that bring people together. High Cotton Brewing Company offers a genuine taste of Memphis hospitality whether you're a craft beer enthusiast or simply looking for a welcoming spot to relax.

**When to Visit:** High Cotton Brewing Company is open throughout the week, with extended hours on weekends. Weekends are livelier, often featuring live music and food trucks.

**Parking:** The brewery offers a small parking lot, which can fill up quickly during peak times. Street parking and pay lots are also available nearby.

**What to Expect:** The taproom at High Cotton has spacious interior and a cozy outdoor patio. The brewery is known for its friendly staff and welcoming vibe. They often host community events and charity fundraisers, adding to the sense of local pride that permeates the space.

A visit to High Cotton Brewing Company offers a chance to experience the rich tradition of craft brewing in Memphis. With its focus on quality, High Cotton provides an authentic and enjoyable setting to explore the city's craft beer offerings.

*High Cotton Brewing*
*https://highcottonbrewing.com/*

After enjoying the diverse offerings from Memphis's thriving brewery scene, it's time to shift gears and dive into the city's distilleries. While the local breweries have crafted a lasting identity with their innovative beers, Memphis's distilleries are making their mark with expertly distilled spirits that reflect the rich heritage and creativity of the city.

# Old Dominick Distillery

Old Dominick Distillery is a proud revival of a historic Memphis brand, originally founded in the late 1800s by Domenico Canale. Reopened in 2017, the distillery brings new life to the Canale family legacy with a range of finely crafted spirits that pay homage to the city's rich history. Located in the heart of downtown Memphis, Old Dominick has quickly become known for its commitment to quality and tradition, producing spirits that embody the spirit of Memphis itself. Their offerings include the Huling Station Straight Bourbon, Memphis Toddy—a unique liqueur inspired by an old family recipe—and Honeybell Vodka, a citrus-infused vodka perfect for mixing.

The distillery combines modern techniques with a profound respect for its roots, offering visitors a glimpse into the art and science of distilling. The spacious facility includes a rooftop bar with stunning views of the Mississippi River, where guests can enjoy not only handcrafted cocktails but also a selection of light bites and snacks. Old Dominick's blend of history and innovation makes it a standout destination for those exploring Memphis's distilleries.

**When to Visit:** Old Dominick Distillery is open for tours and tastings throughout the week, with extended hours on weekends. Weekends offer a more active atmosphere with the possibility of special events.

**Parking:** The distillery offers a small parking lot for visitors, but it can fill up during peak times. Street parking is available nearby, and there are several public parking garages within walking distance.

**What to Expect:** Visitors can enjoy guided tours that provide a behind-the-scenes look at the distilling process, followed by tastings of their signature spirits.

A visit to Old Dominick Distillery offers an opportunity to experience a piece of Memphis history while enjoying expertly crafted spirits. With its blend of tradition and modern flair, along with the option to enjoy the Mississippi River views at the rooftop bar, Old Dominick provides a memorable stop on your journey through the city's craft scene.

*Old Dominick Distillery*
*https://olddominick.com/*

# B.R. Distilling Company
*Blue Note Whiskey*

B.R. Distilling Company is a rising star in the Memphis distillery scene. Founded with a focus on combining traditional distilling methods with modern innovation, B.R. Distilling has quickly gained recognition for crafting high-quality, small-batch spirits that stand out in the competitive world of craft distilling. Blue Note Bourbon, with its smooth finish and complex, full-bodied flavor, has become a favorite among whiskey enthusiasts, including myself, while River Set Rye offers a distinctive, spice-forward profile that adds depth to their lineup.

Located in the heart of Memphis, B.R. Distilling reflects the city's dedication to craft and quality. Their attention to detail and passion for their work is evident in every bottle, making a visit to the distillery a rewarding experience for both whiskey connoisseurs and those new to the world of fine spirits.

> **When to Visit:** B.R. Distilling offers tours and tastings by appointment, allowing for a more personalized experience. Weekdays are typically less busy, offering an intimate look at the distilling process, while weekends may feature special events or promotions.

**Parking:** Parking is generally straightforward at B.R. Distilling, with on-site parking available for visitors. There's also ample street parking in the surrounding area.

**What to Expect:** During your visit, you can expect a guided tour that dives into the history and production techniques behind their bourbons and rye whiskeys. Tastings are offered at the end of the tour, giving you a chance to savor their expertly crafted spirits. The knowledgeable staff is eager to share the story behind each bottle, making the experience both educational and enjoyable.

A visit to B.R. Distilling Company provides an opportunity to explore the craftsmanship behind some of Memphis's finest spirits. With its blend of tradition and innovation, B.R. Distilling offers a glimpse into the art of distilling and the spirit of the city.

*B.R. Distilling*
*https://www.bluenotebourbon.com/*

While exploring the craft breweries and distilleries of Memphis, each stop offers a distinctive and cultural experience. The city's craft beverage scene reflects its creative spirit, where tradition meets innovation in every glass. Whether you're sipping a locally brewed beer or savoring a finely crafted spirit, each establishment provides additional perspective on the artistry and passion that defines Memphis.

These breweries and distilleries are also community hubs where locals and visitors come together to share stories, enjoy live music, and celebrate the city's flavors. The welcoming atmosphere of these venues provides a glimpse into the heart of Memphis's vibrant culture. While visiting restaurants throughout the area, be sure to look for these locally crafted brews and spirits—they're an integral part of the Memphis experience, offering a taste of the city's rich heritage and craftmanship.

With the rich flavors of Memphis's craft brews and spirits still lingering, our journey continues into the heart of the city's cultural landscape. In the next chapter, we'll explore the art, history, and ingenuity that define Memphis beyond its famous music, iconic landmarks and culinary delights.

◆ ◆ ◆

# EXPLORE MEMPHIS

*Art, History, & Culture*

Rich in heritage, Memphis reveals its storied past at every street corner and landmark. While the music and cuisine often take center stage, the city's museums offer an equally compelling journey into its diverse cultural.

For families, there are museums where kids can engage with hands-on exhibits and learn through play. For art lovers, there are spaces that house both timeless masterpieces and contemporary works. And for those interested in the city's industrial past, there are museums that delve into the history of cotton, metalwork, and the ancient peoples that once thrived in this region.

Over the years, I've found myself repeatedly drawn to these museums, each visit offering new insights and greater understanding of the city I call home. Each museum in this chapter is a gateway to understanding the many layers that make Memphis a unique and fascinating destination.

# Museum Of Science & History
## *Pink Palace*

Originally constructed in the 1920s as a mansion for Clarence Saunders, the founder of Piggly Wiggly, the Pink Palace Museums' distinctive pink marble facade is just the beginning of its charm. Today, the Pink Palace is a pillar of Museum of Science & History, offering a diverse range of exhibits that take visitors on a journey through the city's rich history and beyond.

Inside, the museum hosts a variety of permanent and rotating exhibits that chronicle Memphis's evolution—from its early settlement days to its growth as a center of commerce and industry.

The Museum of Science & History is also home to a planetarium and an IMAX theater, where visitors can explore the wonders of space and enjoy visually stunning films. The museum's blend of educational content and engaging presentations makes it a perfect destination for families, history enthusiasts, and anyone curious about the story of Memphis.

> **When to Visit:** The Pink Palace Museum is open daily, with extended hours on certain days for the planetarium and IMAX shows. The annual Crafts Fair is a popular event, so be sure to check the museum's schedule if you're interested in attending.

**Parking:** The museum offers a large, free parking lot for visitors, making it easy to find a spot even on busy days.

**What to Expect:** Visitors can explore the museum's exhibits at their own pace, with plenty of interactive displays to engage children and adults alike. Plan to spend a few hours if you want to see the exhibits, catch a planetarium show, or enjoy an IMAX movie.

The Pink Palace Museum offers a captivating and immersive experience that showcases the spirit of Memphis. Whether you're drawn to its historical exhibits, fascinated by the wonders of the planetarium, or simply looking for a family-friendly destination, the Pink Palace has something to offer everyone. It's a place where the past meets the present, creating an engaging and educational experience for all who visit.

*Pink Palace Museum*
*https://tinyurl.com/pink-palace*

# The Brooks Museum Of Art

The Brooks Museum of Art located in Overton Park, is Memphis's oldest and largest art museum. Established in 1916, it features a diverse collection that ranges from Renaissance masterpieces to contemporary works. The museum is a cultural hub, offering programs like film screenings, art classes, and lectures, making art accessible to all.

Among the museum's most notable exhibits is the European Gallery, which showcases an impressive collection of paintings, including works by artists like Guido Reni and Giovanni Battista Tiepolo. The American Art collection is another must-see, featuring pieces from prominent artists such as Thomas Hart Benton and Childe Hassam, offering a rich tapestry of American culture and history. Visitors can also explore the museum's Sculpture Garden, an outdoor space that harmonizes art with nature, providing a serene setting for reflection and inspiration. The Brooks Museum of Art provides an enriching experience that captures the essence of artistic expression across centuries.

**When to Visit:** Open Tuesday through Sunday check their schedule for special events and exhibitions. Plan your visit around free admission on Wednesday afternoons if you're looking for a budget-friendly option.

**Parking:** Free parking is available behind the museum, with additional street parking in Overton Park. The surrounding park area also offers a pleasant place for a stroll before or after your visit.

**What to Expect:** Spend a few hours exploring the collection and temporary exhibits. The museum also features a café where you can enjoy a meal or snack, as well as a gift shop stocked with art-inspired items.

Looking ahead, the Brooks Museum of Art plans to relocate to a new, state-of-the-art facility in downtown Memphis along the Mississippi River. This move aims to create a stronger connection to the city's cultural life. Until the new facility is ready, the museum will continue operating in its current location, enriching Memphis's cultural landscape and offering an experience that celebrates creativity and artistic expression. As it prepares for its new home, the museum remains a memorable stop for anyone exploring the city's cultural offerings.

*The Brooks Museum of Art*
*https://www.brooksmuseum.org/*

# The Metal Museum
## *Artistry in Metal*

The Metal Museum is a unique destination in Memphis, dedicated entirely to the art and craft of metalwork. Established in 1979, it's the only museum of its kind in the United States, showcasing both contemporary and historic metalwork through a blend of exhibitions, educational programs, and live demonstrations. Situated on a bluff overlooking the Mississippi River, the museum offers visitors an educational experience in a beautifully scenic space. The grounds feature sculptures and stunning river views.

One of the museum's standout features is its blacksmith shop and foundry, where visitors can watch artists at work, bringing traditional techniques to life. The Metal Museum also hosts rotating exhibitions, workshops, and special events, making it a dynamic space for both art lovers and craft enthusiasts.

The Metal Museum offers a wonderful experience for all ages, but it truly comes to life during "Family Fun Days." These free admission events, held twice a year, are packed with kid-friendly activities that engage young visitors in a fun and interactive way.

> **When to Visit:** The Metal Museum is open Tuesday through Sunday. Weekdays offer a quieter experience, while weekends may feature live demonstrations or special events.

**Parking:** Free parking is available on-site, with plenty of space for visitors.

**What to Expect:** Plan to spend a couple of hours exploring the galleries, outdoor sculpture garden, and live demonstrations. The museum shop offers handcrafted items, perfect for picking up a one-of-a-kind souvenir.

The Metal Museum offers something for everyone, providing a distinctive and immersive experience that highlights the artistry and craftsmanship of metalwork. It's a place where tradition meets creativity, set against the backdrop of the Mississippi River, making it a memorable stop on your journey through the city.

 *The Metal Museum*
*https://www.metalmuseum.org/*

# The Cotton Museum

The Cotton Museum, located in the historic Cotton Exchange Building in downtown Memphis, offers a fascinating look into the city's pivotal role in the global cotton industry. Since opening its doors in 2006, the museum has provided visitors with insights into how cotton shaped the history, economy, and culture of Memphis and the surrounding region. The museum's location in the Cotton Exchange Building adds an authentic touch, allowing visitors to step back in time to an era when cotton was king.

The museum's exhibits cover a wide range of topics, from the technical aspects of cotton production to the social and economic impacts of the industry. Visitors can explore the global significance of cotton, as well as its profound effects on the local community. The Cotton Museum also addresses the complex history of the cotton industry, including its ties to slavery and the Civil Rights Movement, offering a comprehensive view of its lasting legacy.

**When to Visit:** The Cotton Museum is open Monday through Saturday. Weekdays are typically quieter, while Saturdays might be busier with tourists.

**Parking:** Paid parking is available in nearby lots and garages, with limited street parking downtown. It's advisable to park in a nearby lot and walk to the museum.

**What to Expect:** Plan to spend an hour or two at the museum. The exhibits are self-guided, allowing you to explore at your own pace. The museum's location makes it easy to combine with other downtown attractions.

The Cotton Museum offers a practical exploration of the industry that played a crucial role in development of Memphis and the surrounding areas, making it a key stop for understanding the economic and cultural forces that have influenced the city. The museum's engaging exhibits make it a family-friendly destination, offering educational experiences that resonate with visitors of all ages. A visit to the Cotton Museum is both educational and a poignant reminder of the complexities of Memphis's past.

*The Cotton Museum*
*https://memphiscottonmuseum.org/*

# C.H. Nash Museum At Chucalissa

The C.H. Nash Museum at Chucalissa offers an opportunity to explore the rich prehistoric Native American culture that once thrived in the Mississippi Valley. Located just outside Memphis, this museum is dedicated to preserving and interpreting the history of the Mississippian period, showcasing artifacts, reconstructed buildings, and exhibits that detail the daily life, traditions, and rituals of the Native American tribes who lived in the region. The museum is situated on a bluff overlooking the Mississippi River, providing a serene and historically significant setting for visitors.

The museum features a variety of exhibits, including an outdoor archaeological site where visitors can see ongoing excavations and learn about the scientific methods used to uncover and study ancient artifacts. Interactive displays and hands-on activities make the C.H. Nash Museum a great destination for families and history enthusiasts alike. The surrounding grounds also include walking trails and outdoor exhibits, offering a peaceful setting to delve into the region's ancient history while enjoying the natural beauty of the area.

**When to Visit:** The museum is open Tuesday through Saturday. Weekdays are usually less crowded, providing a quieter experience, ideal for those who prefer to explore at their own pace.

**Parking:** Free parking is available on-site, with plenty of space for visitors.

**What to Expect:** Plan to spend a few hours exploring the museum and the outdoor archaeological site. Guided tours and special programs are available, so check the schedule if you're interested in a more detailed visit.

With its combination of indoor exhibits, outdoor archaeological sites, and hands-on activities, the museum offers a comprehensive and engaging experience that's perfect for families, history buffs, and anyone interested in the rich Native American heritage of the region. A visit to Chucalissa is a journey back in time, offering valuable insights into the ancient peoples who shaped the history of the Mississippi Valley.

*Chucalissa*
*https://www.memphis.edu/chucalissa/*

# The Children's Museum Of Memphis

The Children's Museum of Memphis (CMOM) is a another popular spot for families, offering interactive, hands-on exhibits that make learning fun for kids. Opened in 1990 and located in Midtown, the museum strives to engage children, with a focus on science, art, and everyday life.

The museum exhibits are educational and entertaining, encouraging children to explore their interests and imaginations. Highlights include the FedEx Aircraft exhibit, where kids can climb into the cockpit of a real plane, and the Supermarket & Diner, where they can play the roles of shoppers, chefs, and servers. The museum also features outdoor attractions like the H2Oh! Splash Park, where children can enjoy interactive water play, and a large Playground equipped with slides, swings, and climbing structures, providing a full day of fun and learning.

One of the museum's most cherished attractions is the Grand Carousel, originally built in 1909 by the Dentzel Carousel Company. This hand-carved wooden carousel operated for many years at the Mid-South Fairgrounds before being carefully dismantled, restored and relocated to CMOM. Reopened in 2017, the carousel is a beautifully preserved piece of Memphis history, offering a nostalgic ride for visitors of all ages.

**When to Visit:** The museum is open daily, with slightly reduced hours on Sundays. Weekends and school holidays are busier, with more programming and activities available.

**Parking:** The museum has a large, free parking lot adjacent to the building, making it convenient for families with young children.

**What to Expect:** Plan to spend a few hours exploring the museum's interactive exhibits, both indoors and outdoors. The museum is designed for children ages 1-10, but there's plenty for the whole family to enjoy.

At the Children's Museum of Memphis, education meets imagination, offering an environment that encourages children to learn through play. Whether your child is an aspiring pilot, a budding artist, or just loves to explore, CMOM provides a rich and engaging experience that the whole family can enjoy. It's a must-visit for families looking to make lasting memories in Memphis.

*Children's Museum of Memphis*
*https://cmom.com/*

Throughout this chapter, I have shown you some of my favorite Memphis museums and revealed the rich tapestry of experiences that await you. Each museum tells a story, connecting you with the city's past, present, and future. These institutions offer profound insights into the forces that have shaped Memphis, whether through hands-on learning for children or explorations of art and history.

Continuing your journey through this incredible city, I encourage you to find time to explore these museums. They are windows into the soul of Memphis, offering experiences that will stay with you long after your trip is over. Each visit is an opportunity to connect with Memphis on a new level, making your time here even more meaningful.

It's time to step off the beaten path. In the next chapter, I'll introduce you to some of the city's lesser-known treasures—places where history, nature, and reflection offer a quieter but equally enriching experience.

# BEYOND THE LANDMARKS

*Off-the-Beaten-Path*

Often celebrated for its moving landmarks, historic music scene, and world-famous barbecue, the city's appeal extends far beyond these well-worn paths. In this chapter, we'll explore some of Memphis's lesser-known treasures—places where history, nature, and reflection intertwine to offer varied connections to the city's diverse character.

From the quiet beauty of Elmwood Cemetery, where the stories of Memphis's past permeate the grounds, to the expansive green haven of Overton Park, these sites provide a respite from the city's bustle and a chance to experience a more tranquil side of Memphis. You'll also discover the Crystal Shrine Grotto, a hidden gem filled with artistry and spirituality, and the Abbey Mausoleum, where a small tribute to Elvis Presley offers a personal connection to the King's legacy.

These off-the-beaten-path locations encourage you to escape the crowds and explore the distinct character of Memphis. Whether you're visiting for the first time or have lived here for years, this chapter will lead you to some of the city's most fascinating and often-overlooked spots.

# Elmwood Cemetery

Elmwood Cemetery is one of Memphis's oldest and most historic cemeteries, offering a serene and poignant glimpse into the city's past. Established in 1852, this 80-acre site is the final resting place for many of Memphis's notable figures, including Civil War soldiers, civil rights leaders, and famous musicians. Wandering through its winding paths, you'll encounter towering trees, elaborate Victorian monuments, and stories etched in stone that speak to the rich history of Memphis.

Elmwood is a beautiful outdoor museum that hosts themed tours and special events throughout the year, each delving into different aspects of Memphis history. The cemetery's tranquil setting and historical significance make it a peaceful retreat from the hustle and bustle of the city, offering a peaceful and reflective experience for visitors.

**When to Visit:** Elmwood Cemetery is open daily, with guided tours available by appointment. Special events and themed tours are also offered throughout the year, so be sure to check the schedule in advance to plan your visit.

**Parking:** Free parking is available on-site, making it easy to access the cemetery.

**What to Expect:** Plan to spend at least an hour exploring the grounds. The cemetery's extensive area can be explored on foot or by car, and the visitors' center provides maps and information to help guide your visit.

Visiting Elmwood Cemetery is a journey through Memphis's past, where the connection to those who shaped the city can be felt. The peaceful atmosphere and historical depth make it a memorable and meaningful stop on any visit to Memphis.

*Elmwood Cemetery*
*https://www.elmwoodcemetery.org/*

# Overton Park

Overton Park is a cherished green space in the heart of Memphis, offering a harmonious blend of natural beauty and historical significance. Established in 1901, this 342-acre park is home to several of Memphis's most beloved attractions, including the Memphis Zoo and the Brooks Museum of Art. While these well-known sites are highlighted in other chapters of this guide, the park itself serves as a peaceful retreat, with lush, forested areas, scenic trails, and open spaces that invite relaxation and exploration.

A key feature of Overton Park is the Old Forest State Natural Area, a rare and protected old-growth forest that provides visitors with a glimpse into the region's natural heritage. The park's history is deeply intertwined with the cultural and social fabric of Memphis, making it not only a place for recreation but also a living historical site that reflects the city's evolution over more than a century.

Another highlight within the park is the Overton Park Shell, a historic outdoor amphitheater where Elvis Presley performed his first paid concert in 1954. Known as one of the birthplaces of rock 'n' roll, the Shell has hosted countless performances over the years, and it continues to be a cherished venue for live music and community events. Check the schedule to find both free and ticketed events from March – September.

**When to Visit:** Overton Park is open daily, with different attractions within the park having their own hours. Early mornings and weekdays are usually quieter, making them ideal times for a peaceful visit, while evenings are often filled with concerts at the Shell.

**Parking:** Parking is available throughout the park, including designated lots near major attractions like the zoo and museum. Street parking is also available but can fill up quickly on weekends.

**What to Expect:** Whether you're looking to explore the trails, visit a museum, or simply relax on the lawn, Overton Park has something for everyone. Plan to spend a few hours or the whole day here, especially if you want to explore multiple areas of the park.

Overton Park is a place where Memphis's natural beauty and rich history converge, offering a peaceful retreat within the city. The park provides a multifaceted experience allowing you to connect with both the city's past and its present in a way that's both relaxing and enriching.

*Overton Park*
*https://overtonpark.org/*

 *Overton Park Shell*
*https://overtonparkshell.org/*

# Martin Music
*The Guitarist's Playground*

If you're a musician or a music lover exploring Memphis, Martin Music is a stop you can't miss. Tucked away in East Memphis, this family-owned guitar shop has been a haven for musicians of all levels since 1971. The store was founded by Jeff Martin, a passionate guitarist who wanted to create a space where musicians could find high-quality instruments and a sense of community. Over the years, Martin Music has become a beloved institution that reflects the rich musical heritage of Memphis.

From its humble beginnings, Martin Music quickly grew into a hub for the city's music scene. Local favorites like Steve Selvidge, guitarist for The Hold Steady and a fixture in Memphis's music community, have been known to frequent the shop. Steve, the son of the legendary Memphis musician Sid Selvidge, often stops by to check out the latest gear, chat with the staff, and connect with fellow musicians. His regular visits underscore the shop's reputation as a trusted spot for quality instruments and a gathering place for Memphis's musical talent.

Martin Music fosters the music community in Memphis. The staff, are always eager to share their expertise, offer advice, or chat about the latest trends in the music world. This welcoming environment has made the store a popular gathering place for Memphis musicians, who come not only to buy gear but also to connect with like-minded individuals who share their love of music.

**When to Visit:** Martin Music is open Monday through Saturday, from 10 AM to 6 PM. Weekdays tend to be quieter, making them a great time to visit if you want to browse or chat with the staff without the weekend rush.

**Parking:** The store has plenty of free parking available in the lot next to the building, making it easy to stop by without worrying about finding a spot.

**What to Expect:** Expect to find a wide range of guitars, amps, and accessories, from vintage treasures to the latest models. The knowledgeable staff is always on hand to offer advice and insights, making it a perfect place to explore whether you're looking to buy or simply soak up some of Memphis's rich musical atmosphere.

Martin Music is the perfect place to immerse yourself in the city's rock 'n' roll spirit. It's a store where history and music come alive, creating an experience that resonates long after you leave. A visit to Martin Music is a step into the heart of Memphis's music scene.

 *Martin Music*
*https://www.martinmusicguitar.com/*

# Crystal Shrine Grotto

Hidden within the Memorial Park Cemetery, the Crystal Shrine Grotto is one of Memphis's most interesting and unexpected attractions. Created by artist Dionicio Rodriguez in the 1930s, this man-made cave features intricate crystal formations and religious scenes. The grotto is a whimsical blend of art and spirituality, making it a fascinating spot for visitors who appreciate the unusual and the artistic.

Surrounded by beautiful gardens and sculptures, the grotto offers a peaceful setting for reflection and exploration. Walking through the grotto's winding paths, explore the various chambers, each with its own theme and set of crystal formations. This site is a testament to the creativity and vision of its creator, providing a tranquil retreat from the hustle and bustle of the city.

> **When to Visit:** The Crystal Shrine Grotto is open daily during cemetery hours. It's a quiet and tranquil spot, making it a good choice for a reflective visit.
>
> **Parking:** Free parking is available within Memorial Park Cemetery, close to the grotto's entrance.
>
> **What to Expect:** Plan to spend about 30 minutes to an hour exploring the grotto and its surrounding gardens. Those who take the time to visit will find a spiritual and inspiring space that offers a glimpse of the city's artistic heritage.

The Crystal Shrine Grotto is a hidden treasure that offers a quiet and meditative experience in the heart of Memphis. This peaceful escape, off the beaten path, is well worth the visit if you're looking to explore one of the city's more unusual settings.

 *Crystal Shrine Grotto*
*https://tinyurl.com/crystal-shrine-grotto*

# The Abbey Mausoleum

Forest Hill Cemetery is home to the Abbey Mausoleum, a lesser-known but fascinating site in Memphis. Built in the early 20th century, the mausoleum features intricate architecture and stained-glass windows, offering a peaceful and contemplative space for visitors. While it may not be on the typical tourist trail, it holds a special place for those interested in the city's history and less visited landmarks.

Of particular interest is a small, fan-created shrine to Elvis Presley, located in the mausoleum where he and his mother, Gladys Presley, were originally interred before being moved to Graceland on October 2, 1977. This quiet tribute is not widely publicized, but for dedicated Elvis fans, it's a meaningful stop where you can leave flowers and mementos, providing a more personal connection with the legacy of the King and his mother.

> **When to Visit:** The mausoleum is open daily, typically from morning until late afternoon.
>
> **Parking:** Free parking is available within the cemetery grounds, close to the mausoleum.
>
> **What to Expect:** Plan to spend about 30 minutes exploring the mausoleum. The site is easy to navigate on your own, and the peaceful atmosphere, combined with the Elvis shrine, is a memorable experience for visitors.

The Abbey Mausoleum offers a quiet, meditative space for those looking for an off-the-beaten-path experience. This hidden gem allows you to experience a more personal side of the city's history.

 *Abbey Mausoleum*
*https://tinyurl.com/abbey-mausoleum*

Walking the serene paths of Elmwood Cemetery, marveling at the artistry of the Crystal Shrine Grotto, or discovering the tranquil beauty of Overton Park will leave a lasting impression and strengthen your appreciation of the city.

So, as you plan your visit to Memphis, consider stepping off the beaten path. Discovering these hidden gems can lead to some of the most cherished memories of your journey.

As we wrap up our exploration of these lesser known spots, it's time to step outside and get active. The next chapter I invite you to discover Memphis's parks, rivers, and trails, where nature provides a perfect blend of adventure and relaxation.

# OUTDOOR ADVENTURE

*Parks, Rivers & Trails*

Where urban life meets the beauty of nature, Memphis offers a diverse array of outdoor spaces that invite exploration, relaxation, and adventure. In this chapter, I will take you to some of Memphis's most cherished green spaces and scenic spots, where the beauty of nature is on full display. Memphis has something for every nature lover and outdoor enthusiast.

This chapter highlights engaging outdoor experiences like the immersive wildlife encounters at the Memphis Zoo and the breathtaking views from Big River Crossing. Each of these locations offers its own distinctive way to connect with the natural world, showcasing the rich landscapes that define the Memphis area. Exploring these parks, rivers, and trails, I think you'll discover that Memphis's outdoor adventures are an integral part of what makes the city so engaging and inviting.

# Shelby Farms Park
## *A Green Oasis*

Shelby Farms Park is one of the largest urban parks in the United States, offering over 4,500 acres of green space and a wide range of outdoor activities for all ages. Located just east of downtown Memphis, this expansive park is a haven for nature lovers, outdoor enthusiasts, and families looking for a day of adventure. The park is a true green oasis, providing a peaceful escape from the city's hustle and bustle.

Shelby Farms Park features a variety of attractions, including over 40 miles of trails for walking, running, and biking, with scenic views of lakes, meadows, and woodlands. The park is home to a herd of buffalo, which roam the wide-open fields, adding to the park's charm. You can also enjoy fishing, or rent various types of paddle boats, such as kayaks, canoes and paddle boards, to explore the park's lakes, or simply relax with a picnic in one of the many shaded areas.

For families, the park offers the Woodland Discovery Playground, a creatively designed play area that encourages exploration and imaginative play. There's also a splash pad for cooling off on hot summer days, as well as horseback riding at the park's stables. Another popular attraction at Shelby Farms is the Go Ape Treetop Adventure course, where visitors can tackle zip lines, rope bridges, and other aerial challenges.

**When to Visit:** Shelby Farms Park is open daily from sunrise to sunset. Weekdays are generally quieter, while weekends are busier with families and outdoor enthusiasts. Special events and festivals often take place in the park, so check the calendar before your visit.

**Parking:** The park has several free parking lots located near the main attractions, making it easy to access different areas of the park.

**What to Expect:** Plan to spend several hours exploring the park, whether you're hiking the trails, enjoying water activities, or just relaxing in the open spaces. The park is also dog-friendly, with a large off-leash area known as The Outback for your furry friends to run and play.

**Amenities**: The park offers restrooms, picnic areas, and rental facilities for bikes and watercraft. Be sure to bring sunscreen and water, especially during the summer months.

Shelby Farms Park offers a perfect blend of natural beauty and recreational activities. Whether you're exploring the Greenline Trail, paddling on the lakes, riding a horse through the trails, or enjoying a concert under the stars, the park provides an unforgettable outdoor experience. It's a place where both locals and visitors can enjoy nature, relax, and create lasting memories.

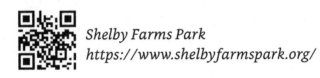

*Shelby Farms Park*
*https://www.shelbyfarmspark.org/*

# The Memphis Zoo

The Memphis Zoo is one of the city's most beloved attractions, offering visitors the chance to see more than 3,500 animals representing over 500 species. Located in Overton Park, the zoo has been a staple of the community since it opened in 1906, providing both entertainment and education to generations of Memphians and visitors alike. The zoo's beautifully landscaped 70-acre grounds are home to a diverse range of habitats, each designed to replicate the natural environments of the animals.

The zoo's exhibits are designed to be both educational and engaging, with highlights like the Kangaroo Experience, where visitors can walk through a free-range area and get up close with red kangaroos. The Teton Trek area is modeled after Yellowstone National Park and features grizzly bears, wolves, and elk, while the Zambezi River Hippo Camp offers a close-up view of hippos, Nile crocodiles, and other African wildlife. The zoo also has a special area for younger visitors, the Once Upon A Farm, where children can interact with farm animals in a hands-on setting.

Throughout the year, the Memphis Zoo hosts a variety of special events, including Zoo Boo, a Halloween celebration, and Zoo Lights, a festive holiday event with light displays and seasonal activities. These events add an extra layer of excitement and make the zoo a must-visit destination any time of the year.

**When to Visit:** The Memphis Zoo is open daily, with extended hours during special events. Weekdays are generally less crowded, making for a more relaxed visit. Spring and fall are ideal times to visit, as the weather is usually mild.

**Parking:** Parking is available in the zoo's dedicated lot for a fee. During peak times, additional parking may be available within Overton Park, but it's best to arrive early if you're looking to avoid the fee based lot.

**What to Expect:** Plan to spend at least a half-day exploring the zoo's exhibits and attractions. The zoo is stroller-friendly and offers several dining options, including cafés and picnic areas. Don't forget to check the daily schedule for animal feedings and keeper talks, which provide an educational and interactive experience for visitors of all ages.

The Memphis Zoo offers an immersive experience that connects visitors with wildlife from around the world. With its diverse exhibits, seasonal events, and educational opportunities, there's always something new and exciting to discover. A visit to the Memphis Zoo provides a perfect blend of adventure, and fun for families, animal lovers, and anyone looking to explore the natural world right in the heart of Memphis.

*The Memphis Zoo*
*https://www.memphiszoo.org/*

# The Mississippi Riverfront

The Mississippi Riverfront is one of Memphis's most scenic areas, offering a blend of natural beauty, history, and recreation. Stretching along the western edge of downtown Memphis, the riverfront provides an ideal place for both locals and visitors to experience the mighty Mississippi River up close. The area features a variety of parks, walking trails, and cultural attractions that highlight the significance of the river in the city's development and identity.

One of the most notable spots along the riverfront is Tom Lee Park, named in honor of Tom Lee, a local African American hero who, in 1925, saved 32 people from drowning after the steamboat M.E. Norman capsized in the river. This park not only commemorates Lee's bravery but also offers a peaceful setting for picnicking, jogging, and enjoying panoramic views of the Mississippi.

Martyr's Park is a serene location dedicated to the memory of those who lost their lives in the 1878 yellow fever epidemic. It's a contemplative space where visitors can reflect on the city's history while taking in the tranquil river views. The Riverwalk, a scenic trail that connects various parts of the riverfront, provides an easy way to explore the area, with markers along the way highlighting the history and significance of the Mississippi River.

**When to Visit:** The Mississippi Riverfront is accessible year-round, with each season offering a different experience. Spring and fall are ideal for enjoying the outdoors, while summer is a good time for a variety of festivals. Early mornings and evenings provide cooler temperatures and stunning views of the river.

**Parking:** Parking is available in several lots along the riverfront. Street parking is also an option, though it can fill up quickly during events.

**What to Expect:** Plan to spend a few hours, or all day, exploring the riverfront's parks, trails, and attractions. The area is great for walking, biking, or simply relaxing by the water.

**Amenities:** The riverfront offers a variety of amenities, including restrooms, picnic areas, and food vendors, particularly during events. Wear comfortable shoes if you plan to explore the Riverwalk, and bring water and sunscreen, especially during the summer months.

The Mississippi Riverfront is a must-visit area in Memphis, offering a range of activities from walking trails to cultural landmarks. With so much to offer let the riverfront be your place to relax, explore, or enjoy a local event. Plan your visit around the parks, trails, and events that interest you most, and take advantage of the amenities and parking options to make the most of your time by the river.

*Mississippi River Front*
*https://www.memphisriverparks.org/*

# Big River Crossing

Big River Crossing is a remarkable feat of engineering and a truly unique attraction for anyone looking to experience the Mississippi River. Stretching nearly a mile in length, this pedestrian and bicycle bridge connects downtown Memphis with West Memphis, Arkansas, making it the longest of its kind across the Mississippi River. Opened in 2016, Big River Crossing offers stunning views of the river and the surrounding landscape, providing both locals and visitors with a scenic route for walking, jogging, and cycling.

The bridge is part of the larger Big River Trail system, which extends for miles into Arkansas, offering outdoor enthusiasts a chance to explore the region's natural beauty. Once across the bridge, you'll find markers and signs that provide information about the river's history, ecology, and its role in shaping the cities along its banks. The experience is particularly captivating at sunset, when the sky and water are painted in bright colors, creating a picturesque backdrop as you cross above the river.

Big River Crossing is also known for its LED light display, which illuminates the bridge at night with a dazzling array of colors and patterns. The lights are often synchronized with special events or holidays, adding an additional flare to the experience. Big River Crossing is a wonderful highlight of the Memphis riverfront.

**When to Visit:** Big River Crossing is open year-round, and its accessible day or night. For the best views and a more comfortable walk or ride, visit during the early morning or late afternoon when the temperatures are cooler, and the lighting is perfect for photos.

**Parking:** Free parking is available at the Martyrs Park lot near the entrance to the bridge on the Memphis side. There's also parking available in West Memphis, making it convenient to start your journey from either side.

**What to Expect:** Plan to spend about an hour crossing the bridge and taking in the sights, although you could easily extend your visit if you explore the trails on the Arkansas side. The bridge is wide with pull-outs along the way, making it suitable for walkers, joggers, cyclists, and sight-seers of all ages. Don't forget your camera to capture the stunning views of the river as you stand over the river looking down from the bridge.

Big River Crossing offers an active and accessible way to experience the Mississippi River, with breathtaking sunsets and panoramic views that capture the essence of the riverfront. The well-maintained paths and convenient parking make it easy to explore, inviting visitors to take their time and enjoy the scenic journey between Memphis, Tennessee and West Memphis, Arkansas. Big River Crossing stands out as a memorable highlight that perfectly blends natural beauty with urban convenience.

*Big River Crossing*
*https://www.bigrivercrossing.com/*

**M**emphis's outdoor spaces offer a variety of ways to enjoy nature, such as exploring trails, relaxing by the river, and taking in the city's scenic views. Each destination in this chapter provides convenient access to recreation and natural beauty, making them great stops if you're looking to get active and enjoy the outdoors in Memphis.

Having explored the natural spaces around town, let's shift our focus to how you can experience Memphis's culture, history, and family-friendly activities in a more structured way. This next chapter isn't meant to be followed with strict adherence but rather to provide themed outlines that spark your imagination as you plan your trip to Memphis. We'll dive into itineraries that blend the best of the city—its music, heritage, and opportunities for adventure—into unforgettable experiences for visitors of all ages.

# ITINERARIES

*MUSIC
CIVIL RIGHTS &
FAMILY ADVENTURE*

This chapter presents three carefully crafted itineraries that guide you through the heart of what will provide lasting memories of your visit to Memphis: its legendary music scene, its profound civil rights heritage, and its active, family-friendly attractions. Each itinerary offers a distinct way to experience the city, allowing you to explore the aspects of Memphis that interest you most.

Each journey is designed to provide an immersive experience and these itineraries make it easy to navigate the city's diverse offerings, ensuring that your experiences in Memphis are enjoyable and meaningful. Please use these itineraries as a starting point, ,but feel free to add or change stops, mix and match days, or combine itineraries to create a visit that's uniquely your own.

# Rhythms Of Memphis Tour

This 3-day itinerary is crafted to immerse you in the city's rich musical heritage. From the soul-stirring sounds of the blues to the birthplace of rock 'n' roll, you'll journey through the heart of Memphis's music scene, discovering the places where legends were born and the sounds that continue to influence generations. This itinerary is designed for music lovers who want to experience the best of Memphis with minimal travel time and maximum enjoyment, offering a seamless blend of history, live performances, and local flavors.

## Day 1: A Day on Beale Street

**Morning:**

> **The Blues Hall of Fame** (1 hour)
> Start your day at The Blues Hall of Fame, where you'll delve into the rich history of the blues and its legendary artists. The museum is packed with memorabilia, albums, and exhibits that celebrate the pioneers of this influential genre, offering you a view to the roots of the blues.
>
> **Stax Museum of American Soul Music** (1.5 hours)
> After visiting The Blues Hall of Fame, head over to the Stax Museum of American Soul Music. Located at the original site of Stax Records, this museum offers an in-depth look at the soul music movement and its impact on the world. Explore exhibits dedicated to stars like Otis Redding and Isaac Hayes and learn about the

legacy of soul music in Memphis.

**Lunch:**

**Blues City Café** (On Beale Street)
Enjoy a classic Memphis meal at Blues City Café, located right on Beale Street. Famous for its ribs, catfish, and Southern sides, this spot is perfect for refueling before exploring the rest of Beale Street.

**Afternoon:**

**Beale Street** (2 hours or more)
Spend your afternoon wandering Beale Street, the heart of Memphis's blues scene. Visit spots like B.B. King's Blues Club, and let the live music pouring out of the bars and clubs set the mood. Be sure to check out A. Schwab and grab a malt at the nostalgic soda fountain. Beale Street is not just a destination; it's an experience that embodies the soul of Memphis.

**Dinner:**

**Itta Bena** (Above B.B. King's Blues Club)
Dine at Itta Bena, offering Southern-inspired dishes in a cozy, upscale setting right on Beale Street. This hidden gem above B.B. King's Blues Club combines great food with a relaxing atmosphere, making it a perfect spot to unwind after an afternoon on Beale Street.

*For a more budget-friendly option,:* **B.B. King's Blues Club** downstairs offers a lively atmosphere with a menu of Southern comfort food.

**Evening:**

### Live Music on Beale Street

After dinner, feel free to stay on Beale if you want to watch the crowd grow and volume rise, Beale street truly comes to life at night. Whether it's blues, rock, or jazz, there's something for every music lover here.

## Day 2: A Day with the King

**Morning:**

**Sun Studio** (2 hours)

Begin your day at Sun Studio, the birthplace of rock 'n' roll, where legends like Elvis Presley, Johnny Cash, and Jerry Lee Lewis recorded their first hits. A guided tour will walk you through the history of rock 'n' roll and provide a close-up look at the studio that shaped the sound of a generation.

**Lunch:**

**Huey's** (Downtown)
After your visit to Sun Studio, head to Huey's, a Memphis favorite known for its burgers and laid-back atmosphere. This casual spot is perfect for a quick and satisfying meal before continuing your rock 'n' roll journey.

**Afternoon:**

**Graceland** (2.5 hours)
Spend the afternoon at Graceland, the home of Elvis Presley. Explore the mansion where the King lived, visit the Elvis Presley Car Museum, and pay your respects at the Meditation Garden, where Elvis is laid to rest. Graceland offers an immersive look into the life and legacy of the King of Rock 'n' Roll.

**Dinner:**

**Second Line** (Overton Square)
End your day with a meal at Second Line, located in the heart of Overton Square. Chef Kelly English's New Orleans-inspired cuisine offers a delicious and relaxed dining experience.

*A less expensive option:* **Young Avenue Deli** offers a casual atmosphere with a diverse menu and is just a short drive from Overton Square.

**Evening:**

**Lafayette's Music Room** (Overton Square)
Cap off your day with a trip to Lafayette's Music Room in Overton Square for live music in a laid-back atmosphere. This historic venue hosts a variety of local and touring acts, offering a great way to experience the Memphis music scene.

## Day 3: A Day of Legendary Music

**Morning:**

### Memphis Rock 'n' Soul Museum (2 hours)
In the morning head over to the Memphis Rock 'n' Soul Museum, where you'll dive into the rich history of Memphis music. This museum explores the origins of rock and soul music, tracing their roots from the rural origins of sharecroppers to the influential sounds that shaped the music industry.

### Memphis Music Hall of Fame (1 hour)
Just around the corner from the Rock 'n' Soul Museum, the Memphis Music Hall of Fame celebrates the legends who put Memphis on the musical map. Explore exhibits that honor musical artists like Elvis Presley, B.B. King, and Justin Timberlake, and gain insight into the individuals who helped shape the city's musical legacy.

**Lunch:**

### Arcade Restaurant (South Main District)
Enjoy lunch at the Arcade Restaurant, Memphis's oldest café, known for its classic diner fare and historic charm. This throwback spot offers a nostalgic experience with its retro decor and a menu filled with Southern comfort food.

### Afternoon:

**Overton Park Shell** (1.5 hours)
Spend your afternoon at the Overton Park Shell, the historic outdoor venue where Elvis Presley performed his first paid concert. The Shell often hosts free concerts and events, making it a perfect spot to relax and soak in the musical heritage of Memphis. Even if there's no performance during your visit, it's a great spot to relax, soak in the atmosphere, and reflect on the musical heritage that resonates from this historic venue.

**Overton Square** (2-5 hours)
After taking in the history at Overton Park Shell, head back to Overton Square, a lively district known for its local atmosphere and array of live music venues. With a variety of spots offering everything from blues to jazz and rock, Overton Square is a great place to experience Memphis's musical diversity in a more contemporary setting.

### Dinner:

**Soul Fish** (Cooper St.)
End your day with a meal at Soul Fish, a beloved local spot known for its Southern-inspired dishes and welcoming atmosphere. The menu features classics like fried catfish and po'boys, offering a taste of Memphis comfort food.

This 3-day Memphis music journey offers an in-depth exploration of the city's rich musical heritage. Visiting iconic sites, experiencing live performances, and walking in the footsteps of legends, you'll gain a deeper understanding of how Memphis shaped the sounds that continue to influence music today. I've designed this itinerary to leave you with lasting memories and a genuine connection to the rhythms and stories that make Memphis such a critical part of American music history.

◆ ◆ ◆

# Memphis Civil Rights Experience

Memphis played a pivotal role in the American Civil Rights Movement, serving as a battleground for the struggle for justice, equality, and human rights. This 2-day itinerary is designed to guide you through the city's most significant civil rights landmarks, where history was made and where the legacies of those who fought for freedom continue to inspire.

**Day 1: A Legacy of Leadership**

**Morning:**

**National Civil Rights Museum at the Lorraine Motel** (2.5 hours)

Begin your journey at the National Civil Rights Museum, located at the historic Lorraine Motel where Dr. Martin Luther King Jr. was tragically assassinated while fighting for just treatment and basic protections for Memphis sanitation workers. The museum offers a comprehensive look at the Civil Rights Movement, from the era of slavery through to the ongoing fight for justice. This powerful and educational experience sets a reflective tone for your tour, immersing you in the struggles and triumphs of the movement.

**Lunch:**

**Central BBQ** (Near the National Civil Rights Museum)
After your museum visit, enjoy a signature Memphis meal at Central BBQ, just a short walk away. Known for its slow-smoked meats, delicious sides, and friendly atmosphere, Central BBQ is a local favorite and a perfect spot to relax and recharge for the afternoon.

**Afternoon:**

**Beale Street Baptist Church** (1 hour)
Visit Beale Street Baptist Church, one of the oldest African American churches in Memphis. This historic church played a crucial role as a hub for civil rights organizing and remains an important site for those interested in the history of the movement.

**Mason Temple** (1 hour)
Next, head to Mason Temple, where Dr. Martin Luther King Jr. delivered his prophetic "Mountaintop" speech on the night before his assassination. The temple stands as a powerful testament to his enduring legacy and the ongoing struggle for equality. Visiting this site offers a moving connection to one of the most significant moments in civil rights history.

**Dinner:**

### Blues City Café

End your day with a satisfying southern meal at Blues City Café, located right on the iconic Beale Street. Known for its mouthwatering southern comfort food, Blues City Café is famous for its BBQ ribs, catfish, and hearty sides like baked beans and coleslaw. The upbeat atmosphere, complete with live music performances most nights, makes it the perfect spot to soak in the local culture while enjoying a delicious dinner.

***Beale Street*** *(Optional) If you're in the mood for more after dinner, continue your night with live music at one of the many clubs along Beale Street. The street comes alive in the evening with a mix of blues, jazz, and rock, offering a uplifting end to your first day.*

## Day 2: The Fight for Equality

**Morning:**

**Elmwood Cemetery: Civil Rights Leaders Tour** (1.5 hours)

Head over to Elmwood Cemetery, exploring the lives and legacies of civil rights leaders and the other significant figures buried here. The cemetery offers self-guided and guided tours that provide a more in-depth perspective on the history of the Civil Rights Movement in Memphis.

**Clayborn Temple** (1 hour)

Before lunch stop by Clayborn Temple, a historic site that played a pivotal role during the 1968 Sanitation Workers' Strike. Just outside the temple, you'll find the I Am A Man Plaza, dedicated to the courage of the striking workers and their fight for dignity and equality. The plaza and temple together offer a powerful connection to the history of the Civil Rights Movement.

**Lunch:**

**The Four Way** (Downtown)

Enjoy lunch at The Four Way, a historic soul food restaurant that has served as a gathering place for civil rights leaders and locals alike.

**Afternoon:**

> **The Cotton Museum** (1.5 hours)
> Spend your afternoon at the Cotton Museum, housed in the historic Cotton Exchange Building. The museum offers a fascinating exploration of the cotton industry's impact on Memphis, its economy, and its ties to the history of slavery and the Civil Rights Movement. The exhibits walk you through the industry's influence on the city's development and its role in shaping the broader social and economic landscape.

**Dinner:**

> **Char** (Midtown)
> End your day with dinner at Char, a stylish spot in Midtown known for its Southern cuisine with a modern twist. Whether you're in the mood for a steak, seafood, or a classic Southern dish, Char offers a refined dining experience in a relaxed setting.
>
> *A less expensive option:* **The BBQ Shop** offers award-winning Memphis barbecue in a casual atmosphere, don't forget to try the signature barbecue spaghetti.
>
> ***Lafayette's Music Room** (Optional)*
> *After dinner, consider heading to Lafayette's Music Room in Overton Square for live music in a laid-back atmosphere. This venue is a great place to unwind with some of the best local and touring acts.*

I hope this This 2-day itinerary delivers a meaningful and educational experience, connecting you with the powerful history of the Civil Rights Movement in Memphis. Through visits to key sites and local landmarks, you'll gain a profound understanding of the city's critical role in this pivotal chapter of American history, leaving you with lasting impressions and a stronger bond to the struggle for justice and equality.

# Memphis Family Days

A city filled with opportunities for families to learn, play, and explore together, Memphis offers so much for so many. This 3-day itinerary is designed to provide a perfect blend of fun and education, ensuring that both kids and adults have a memorable experience. Each day combines interactive learning with exciting activities, creating a journey that's both enriching and entertaining. Whether you're exploring the wonders of science, diving into history, or enjoying the great outdoors, "Memphis Family Days" is your guide to an unforgettable family adventure in the Bluff City.

**Day 1: Interactive Learning**

**Morning:**

> **The Children's Museum of Memphis** (2 hours)
> Start your family adventure at The Children's Museum of Memphis, where kids can dive into hands-on learning experiences. The museum is packed with interactive exhibits that explore science, art, and history in a fun and engaging way. Highlights include a real airplane cockpit, a splash park, and an imaginative grocery store exhibit. It's the perfect place to spark curiosity and creativity in young minds.

**Lunch:**

**Huey's** (Midtown)
Head over to Huey's, a Memphis favorite known for its burgers and laid-back atmosphere. The midtown location is only 5 minutes from the Children's Museum. This casual spot is perfect for a quick and satisfying meal before heading to the Zoo.

**Afternoon:**

**Memphis Zoo** (3 hours)
Spend your afternoon exploring the Memphis Zoo, one of the city's most beloved attractions. Home to over 3,500 animals, the zoo features exhibits like the Teton Trek and Zambezi River Hippo Camp, offering plenty to see and do. Don't miss the Kangaroo Experience, where kids can get up close to these fascinating creatures. The Memphis Zoo provides both education and excitement, making it a great family destination.

**Dinner:**

**Bayou Grill** (Overton Square)
End your day with dinner at Bayou Grill, where the menu offers a variety of Cajun and Creole dishes in a lively, family-friendly setting. From jambalaya to po'boys, there's something for everyone, ensuring a delicious and satisfying end to your first day of exploration.

## Day 2: Art and Exploration

**Morning:**

**The Metal Museum** (1.5-3 hours)
Start your day at the Metal Museum, where art and history come alive through the fascinating world of metalwork. Explore galleries filled with intricate pieces, from jewelry to large-scale sculptures, and don't miss the chance to watch live demonstrations in the blacksmith shop and foundry. If you're visiting during "Family Fun Days," kids can enjoy hands-on activities, games, and educational programming tailored just for them. The museum's beautiful riverside grounds are perfect for a leisurely walk before heading to lunch.

**Lunch:**

**Loflin Yard** (Near downtown)
After exploring the Metal Museum, head to Loflin Yard for a laid-back lunch in a family-friendly outdoor setting. With plenty of open space, picnic tables, and lawn games, it's a great spot for kids to play while the whole family enjoys casual fare in a relaxed atmosphere.

**Afternoon:**

### Pink Palace Museum (2.5 hours)

After lunch head over to the Pink Palace Museum, which offers a mix of history, science, and cultural exhibits. The museum is home to a planetarium, an IMAX theater, and the historic Pink Palace Mansion. There's something for everyone here, making it an educational yet entertaining stop that will captivate both children and adults.

**Dinner:**

### Young Avenue Deli (Cooper Young)

End your day with dinner at Young Avenue Deli, a popular spot known for its relaxed atmosphere and diverse menu. With options ranging from burgers and sandwiches to vegetarian dishes, it's a great place for families to unwind after a day full of exploration.

## Day 3: Science and Adventure

**Morning:**

### C.H. Nash Museum at Chucalissa (2 hours)
Start your final day with a visit to the C.H. Nash Museum at Chucalissa, where families can explore Native American history and archaeology. The museum offers hands-on exhibits and outdoor activities, such as a nature trail and an archaeological dig site, making it both educational and engaging for kids.

**Lunch:**

### Elwood's Shack (On the way to Shelby Farms Park)
Stop for lunch at Elwood's Shack, a hidden gem known for its delicious sandwiches and casual vibe. It's a great spot to refuel before heading to the park. With its laid-back atmosphere and hearty menu, Elwood's Shack offers a satisfying meal to keep the family energized for the afternoon.

**Afternoon:**

### Shelby Farms Park (3 hours or more)
Spend your afternoon at Shelby Farms Park, one of the largest urban parks in the country. The park offers a wide range of activities, including paddle boating, biking, and the Woodland Discovery Playground. Go horseback riding, view the buffalo herd or check out the zip line, Go Ape Treetop Adventure Course. It's the perfect place for children to burn off energy and for families to enjoy the great outdoors together.

**Dinner:**

**Railgarten** (Cooper-Young)
End your day at Railgarten, a family-friendly spot that combines dining with outdoor fun. With its eclectic menu, playgrounds, and live music, Railgarten offers something for everyone. It's a lively and relaxing place to wrap up your Memphis family adventure.

This Memphis Family Days itinerary provides a well-rounded mix of activities that are both fun and educational. Over these three days, you'll have explored interactive museums, enjoyed outdoor adventures, and experienced the rich history and culture of Memphis. This itinerary is designed to keep kids engaged while offering plenty of opportunities for family bonding. You'll leave having experienced what makes Memphis a great destination for families, along with memories that will last long after your trip.

# CONCLUSION

As we conclude this journey through Memphis, I hope you've found yourself captivated by the sounds, history and cuisine that define the city. From its musical roots to its pivotal role in the fight for civil rights, Memphis offers a tapestry of experiences that provide amazing perspective on some of the critical events and influences that have shaped the country.

Throughout this guide, we've explored Memphis in all its dimensions—walking through its legendary streets, delving into its flavorful cuisine, and discovering the creativity that pulses through its art and craft scenes. I've carefully written each chapter to showcase the city's highlights and provide an understanding of the history and culture that make Memphis far more than just a destination. Instead of a place to get away, this is a place to dive into.

Memphis invites you to engage all your senses. Here, music isn't just heard; it's felt in the soul. Food isn't just tasted; it tells a story with every bite. History isn't just learned; it's experienced in the places where it unfolded. Whether you came to Memphis for the music, the food, the history, or simply to explore something new, I hope this guide enriches your experience and helps you see the city through the eyes of someone who's been touched by its charm and complexity.

As you continue your exploration of Memphis, take with you the understanding that this city is alive with stories — stories of struggle, triumph, creativity, and resilience.

The places you've visited are just the beginning. There's always more to uncover, more to experience, and more to love about Memphis.

This is a city that doesn't just invite you to visit; it invites you to become a part of its ongoing story. As you carry these memories with you, I hope you'll feel a lasting connection to Memphis and all it has to offer.

If you have not already done so, please consider leaving a review on Amazon for this book. Your review helps support my interests in bringing you additional titles as well as making this guide easier to find for others looking to explore this great city.

 *Amazon Link: Memphis Travel Guide https://www.amazon.com/dp/B0DGTS1CH8/*

❖ ❖ ❖

# RESOURCES

**A. Schwab**. (n.d.). *A. Schwab*. https://www.a-schwab.com/
**Arcade Restaurant**. (n.d.). *The Arcade Restaurant*. https://arcaderestaurant.com/
**Beale Street**. (n.d.). *Beale Street: Home of the Blues*. https://bealestreet.com/
**Blues City Café**. (n.d.). *Blues City Café*. https://bluescitycafé.com/
**Blues Foundation**. (n.d.). *Blues Hall of Fame Museum*. https://blues.org/hall-of-fame-museum/
**Blue Note Bourbon**. (n.d.). *B.R. Distilling Company (Blue Note Bourbon)*. https://www.bluenotebourbon.com/
**Brooks Museum of Art**. (n.d.). *The Brooks Museum of Art*. https://www.brooksmuseum.org/
**Central BBQ**. (n.d.). *Central BBQ*. https://eatcbq.com/
**Children's Museum of Memphis**. (n.d.). *Children's Museum of Memphis (CMOM)*. https://cmom.com/
**ChatGPT**. (2024). Assistance provided by ChatGPT (Version GPT-4) in the development of Memphis Travel Guide. OpenAI.
**Char Memphis**. (n.d.). *Char Memphis*. https://memphis.charrestaurant.com/
**Civil Rights Trail**. (n.d.). *Civil Rights Trail*. https://civilrightstrail.com/
**Crosstown Concourse**. (n.d.). *Crosstown Concourse*. https://crosstownconcourse.com/
**Earnestine & Hazel's**. (n.d.). *Earnestine & Hazel's*. https://www.earnestineandhazel.com/
**Elmwood Cemetery**. (n.d.). *Elmwood Cemetery*. https://www.elmwoodcemetery.org/
**Elwood's Shack**. (n.d.). *Elwood's Shack*. https://www.elwoodsshack.com/
**Find A Grave**. (n.d.). *Virtual Cemetery: Abbey Mausoleum*. https://www.findagrave.com/virtual-cemetery/122422?page=2#sr-54473788
**Four Way Restaurant**. (n.d.). *The Four Way*. https://www.fourway901.com/
**Ghost River Brewing Co.**. (n.d.). *Ghost River Brewing Company*. https://www.ghostriverbrewing.com/
**Graceland**. (n.d.). *Graceland: The Home of Elvis Presley*. https://www.graceland.com/
**Green Beetle**. (n.d.). *The Green Beetle*. https://www.thegreenbeetle.com/
**Gus's World Famous Fried Chicken**. (n.d.). *Gus's Fried Chicken*. https://www.gusfriedchicken.com/
**High Cotton Brewing Co.**. (n.d.). *High Cotton Brewing Company*. https://highcottonbrewing.com/
**Huey's**. (n.d.). *Huey's: Home of the Huey Burger*. https://hueyburger.com/
**Loflin Yard**. (n.d.). *Loflin Yard*. https://www.loflinyard.com/
**Majestic Grille**. (n.d.). *The Majestic Grille*. https://www.majesticgrille.com/

Mason Temple. (n.d.). *The Famous Lorraine Motel.* https://www.civilrightsmuseum.org/news/posts/the-famous-lorraine-motel

Memorial Park Cemetery. (n.d.). *Crystal Shrine Grotto.* https://www.memorialparkfuneralandcemetery.com/locations/crystal-shrine-grotto

Memphis Cotton Museum. (n.d.). *The Cotton Museum.* https://memphiscottonmuseum.org/

Memphis Made Brewing Co.. (n.d.). *Memphis Made Brewing Company.* https://www.memphismadebrewing.com/

Memphis Pink Palace Museum. (n.d.). *Pink Palace Museum.* https://moshmemphis.com/exhibits-collections/pink-palace-mansion/

Memphis Rock 'n' Soul Museum. (n.d.). *Rock 'n' Soul Museum.* https://www.memphisrocknsoul.org/

Memphis River Parks Partnership. (n.d.). *The Mississippi Riverfront.* https://www.memphisriverparks.org/

Memphis River Parks Partnership. (n.d.). *Big River Crossing.* https://www.bigrivercrossing.com/

Memphis Zoo. (n.d.). *Memphis Zoo.* https://www.memphiszoo.org/

Mollie Fontaine Lounge. (n.d.). *Mollie Fontaine Lounge.* https://molliefontainelounge.com/

Mud Island River Park. (n.d.). *Mud Island River Park.* https://memphisriverparks.org/

National Civil Rights Museum. (n.d.). *National Civil Rights Museum at the Lorraine Motel.* https://www.civilrightsmuseum.org/

Overton Park Conservancy. (n.d.). *Overton Park.* https://overtonpark.org/

Payne's Bar-B-Q. (n.d.). *Payne's Bar-B-Q.* https://www.paynesbbq.com/

Restaurant Iris. (n.d.). *Restaurant Iris.* https://www.restaurantiris.com/

Second Line. (n.d.). *Second Line.* https://www.secondlinememphis.com/

Shelby Farms Park. (n.d.). *Shelby Farms Park.* https://www.shelbyfarmspark.org/

Soul Fish Café. (n.d.). *Soul Fish Café.* https://soulfishcafé.com/

Stax Museum of American Soul Music. (n.d.). *Stax Museum.* https://staxmuseum.org/

Sun Studio. (n.d.). *Sun Studio.* https://www.sunstudio.com/

The Bar-B-Q Shop. (n.d.). *The Bar-B-Q Shop.* https://thebar-b-qshop.com/

The Beauty Shop. (n.d.). *The Beauty Shop Restaurant.* https://thebeautyshoprestaurant.com/

The Cupboard Restaurant. (n.d.). *The Cupboard Restaurant.* https://www.thecupboardrestaurant.com/

Uncle Lou's Fried Chicken. (n.d.). *Uncle Lou's Fried Chicken.* https://www.unclelousfriedchicken.com/

Wiseacre Brewing Co.. (n.d.). *Wiseacre Brewing Company.* https://wiseacrebrew.com/

*These references have been used to provide accurate and helpful information throughout this guide, ensuring that your experience in Memphis is as enriching and enjoyable as possible.*